The Best
125 Meatless
Pasta Dishes

The Best 125 Meatless Pasta Dishes

Mindy Toomay
and
Susann Geiskopf-Hadler

SOUVENIR PRESS

Cook's Vow

Tomato, supple and serene,
offers itself to the sauce.
And just for a moment
I feel it. Surrender so deep:
full, ripe willingness
to transform.

I vow to work with the courage of flowers
opening,
as true to myself as an apple,
bright red.

Dusk paints its blush on my apron.
There are friends in the house
to be fed.

Mindy Toomay

Acknowledgments

Everyone who helped to make me helped to make this book, and I appreciate you all. A very special thanks goes to my mother, the late Edith M. Cunningham Lackey, for being a wonderful model of creative cooking. Thank you to Lynn Hager, whose enthusiasm and expertise helped to fuel the first round of recipe production. Thanks to Ben Davis Jr., my way-back and still-going-strong vegetarian cooking comrade. And thanks especially to my neglected husband, Tad Toomay, and his sister Claire Toomay, long-suffering house-mates who were forced to devour pound after pound of pasta during the development of this book. Indeed, thanks to the smiling parade of tasters that flowed through our house for months. You shall remain nameless here, but not forgotten (those who did dishes are sure to be richly rewarded in the afterlife). And a hearty thanks to the folks at Prima Publishing—particularly our editor, Jennifer Basye—for their energy, encouragement, and good cheer throughout the process. May we all continue to nourish each other.

Mindy Toomay

Fresh ingredients are inspiring and become the catalyst to creating delicious meals. My life is full of travel, which allows me to sample foods from many continents. I want to thank my mother the late Jill Crampton Geiskopf, and my father, Earl Geiskopf, for instilling in me that sense of travel, and for giving me the confidence that I can succeed. Having an idea, then bringing it to life, is a wonderful accomplishment. I thank my husband, Guy Hadler, for growing so many vegetables and herbs for our table, and for being such an appreciative eater over the years. I would like to acknowledge Bunnie Day; she is a constant support person. I thank Lori Shull, my business associate, for running the business while I devoted my time to this book. My friend Linda Flamm, a self-proclaimed novice cook, helped to kitchen-test the recipes with very successful results! Thank you, Linda. Elizabeth Blaise has contributed creative ideas to the project, which have been well appreciated. To all of my dinner guests, thank you for eating and enjoying my creations. To the staff at Prima Publishing, and readers everywhere, I hope you enjoy creating these delicious, nutritious pasta recipes in your kitchen.

Susann Geiskopf-Hadler

Conversion Tables

When measuring out the ingredients for the recipes it is important to note that the 'cup' measurements refer to American cups which are smaller than the standard British cup. (1 US cup = 8fl oz; 1 UK cup = 10fl oz.) Where ingredients are measured in tablespoons and teaspoons, please note that they refer to the American measures which again are slightly smaller than the British.

Cup Measurements

Cup	Imperial	Metric
¼ cup	2fl oz	60ml
⅓ cup	3fl oz	84ml
½ cup	4fl oz	125ml
⅔ cup	5fl oz	170ml
¾ cup	6fl oz	185ml
1 cup	8fl oz	250ml
1 cup flour	4oz	100g
1 cup sugar	8 oz	225g

Length

Imperial	Metric
1 inch	2.5cm
2 inches	5.1cm
3 inches	7.6cm
4 inches	10.2cm
5 inches	12.7cm
6 inches	15.3cm
8 inches	20.4cm
10 inches	25.4cm
1 foot (12 inches)	30.6cm

Weight

Imperial	Metric
1oz	25g
2oz	50g
4oz	100g
8oz	225g
1lb (16oz)	450g

Liquid Measures

Imperial	Metric
1fl oz	28.4ml
35fl oz	1 litre
¼ pint	150ml
½ pint	300ml
¾ pint	600ml

Oven Temperatures

Regulo	Fahrenheit	Celsius
¼	225°	110°
½	250°	130°
1	275°	140°
2	300°	150°
3	325°	165°
4	350°	180°
5	375°	190°
6	400°	200°
7	425°	220°
8	450°	230°
9	475°	240°

✔ Almost Instant Recipes

Almost Instant Recipes

Contents

✔ Almost Instant

Vegetable-Based Stovetop Sauces   126

Baked and Stuffed Pasta   257

Introduction

Passion for pasta is an insatiable affair. To satisfy our hunger for simple, substantial nourishment, we turn again and again to pasta. How can a humble paste of flour and water inspire such devotion?

Perhaps we love it because it combines so deliciously with so many foods: mushrooms and garlic, vegetables and nuts, cheese and tomatoes, a gardenful of herbs. Whether hot or cold, whether sparsely or luxuriously dressed, the unpretentious character of pasta is endearing. What's more, most pasta dishes are quick and easy to prepare—they fit nicely into the puzzle of our busy lives. (Look for the Almost Instant designation on some recipes—they are particularly fast and easy to prepare.) Also to its credit, pasta is economical and nutritious. Health experts tell us to derive the greatest portion of our calories from complex carbohydrates, and pasta fills the bill. Those who have thought healthy food can't be delicious should reconsider.

Many pasta shapes and flavors inhabit this book, combined with a world of seasonings. Indian curry and the chilies of Mexico are as comfortable on a bed of noodles as the Sicilian olive is. So our out-of-the-ordinary dishes celebrate the cuisine of many nations, sometimes in unorthodox combinations.

Tradition has not been utterly abandoned. She hovers near the pantry, responding wisely to our queries but forbidden to meddle. Originality prevails in our kitchens—that is the fun and fulfillment of cooking!

Putting Together Your Creative Pasta Kitchen

A Well-Stocked Pasta Pantry

In addition to many shapes and sizes of dried pasta and an abundance of fresh vegetables, the well-stocked pasta kitchen contains a selection of the following essentials.

Cooking Oils and Butter

The oil of choice for most pasta cooks is extra virgin olive oil. The pure essence of the olive, obtained from the fruit's initial pressing without the use of chemicals, it has a robust olive aroma and flavor that perfectly complement tomatoes, mushrooms, herbs, and other classic pasta partners. Extra virgin olive oil is flavorful enough to be a sauce unto itself, with few and simple additions like garlic, herbs, and cheese (for instance, Poppy Seed Noodles on page 129).

For certain purposes, low-calorie canola oil (also known as rapeseed oil) is a good substitute for olive oil. It tastes bland and unobtrusive, so it will not overpower a dish with an unwanted flavor. On the other hand, it won't contribute anything worthwhile to the flavor of a savory dish, as olive oil will. If you have fat-related health concerns, use canola oil when it seems appropriate. (Because of its blandness, we recommend you do not use canola oil in salad dressings.)

Other oils are occasionally preferred. In stir-frying ingredients for an Asian-style pasta, you may wish to use peanut oil, which tolerates high heat without smoking or burning. Also useful for Asian cooking and suggested in a few recipes in this book is roasted sesame oil, pressed from toasted sesame seeds. Its dark, smoky flavor is unique and quite delicious.

In some recipes, butter seems the natural choice. Cream sauces, for instance, usually begin with at least a little butter, and curry dishes traditionally use clarified butter rather than oil as a starting point. We prefer the unsalted variety for its purity and sweetness.

Those who count calories or cholesterol can usually reduce the amount of oil or butter called for in a recipe without disastrous results. Steaming onion, garlic, and spices in a few tablespoons of water before other ingredients are added is a fine alternative to the traditional oil or butter sauté, particularly in tomato-based and vegetable-based sauces.

Wines and Spirits

In moderation, fermented grape and grain beverages have a place in our diet. We find many culinary uses for certain types of alcohol, as well as enjoying wine as a refreshing libation with food.

In particular, you will note the use of port, sherry (both sweet and dry), and Madeira wines, and occasionally brandy, in our recipes. Mirin, a sweet rice wine from Asia, also makes several appearances. You can substitute sweet sherry if you don't have mirin on hand. The amounts used are not great, so the quantity of alcohol in each serving is negligible. The chemical composition of alcoholic beverages is altered by the cooking process, so foods containing them will not carry the alcohol bite some people find unpleasant.

Because the flavors of these wines and spirits are distinctive and essential to certain dishes, we suggest that those who object to their use simply bypass the recipes containing them.

Tomatoes

Tomatoes in all their variety are important pasta partners. Keep canned whole tomatoes, tomato puree, stewed tomatoes, crushed tomatoes, and tomato paste on hand. They make fine sauces when good fresh tomatoes aren't available.

Dried tomatoes, now widely available, have inspired many a recipe in this book. When dried, tomatoes develop a chewiness and robust meaty flavor that is quite distinctive. Dried tomatoes can be purchased at some natural food markets in bulk or at well-stocked supermarkets in cellophane packages. They can also be found marinating in olive oil at your local Italian delicatessen. Marinated dried tomatoes can be costly, but a little goes a long way. Of course, the paper-dry variety can be stored in olive oil at home to achieve a texture similar to that

of the gourmet Italian kind. Briefly immerse the dried tomatoes in boiling water, drain well, cover with extra virgin
olive oil, and store in a closed container in the cupboard. The
oil from the tomatoes can be used with delicious results in
many recipes that call for olive oil.

Fresh tomatoes during their peak summer season make a
light and flavorful pasta topping—whether cooked or raw—
with the addition of only a few other ingredients. Grow your
own in a pot on the porch if you have no garden plot, just to experience perfect tomato flavor and texture. Supermarket tomatoes take a poor second place in quality. If you must resort to
marginally ripe supermarket tomatoes, buy them a couple of
days in advance and ripen them in a basket at room temperature. Except when locally grown and purchased at the height of
summer, tomatoes may not convey the characteristic sweetness prized by Italian cooks. Sometimes a little sugar is added
to remedy this situation. Keep this in mind if the acidity of your
tomato sauce needs a little mellowing.

Garlic and Ginger

What can we say about garlic? You must love it to be considered
a true pasta aficionado. Its pungent punch defines many classic
pasta preparations. There are those who love pasta dressed
only in a sprinkling of Parmesan cheese, perhaps a little fresh
parsley, and a large quantity of minced garlic sautéed in butter
or olive oil.

Fresh garlic is sold in bulbs, just as they come from the
ground (though cleaned up a bit and with stalks removed). The
bulb should be firm when you squeeze it. Garlic that is past its
prime will dry and shrivel in the paper skin and you will notice
this when you test the bulb. Store garlic bulbs in a dry, airy
spot. Individual cloves are removed from the bulb, crushed
gently with the side of a broad knife blade to separate the paper
skin, and put through a press or finely minced with a sharp

knife. As a rule of thumb, an average-size garlic clove yields about 1 teaspoon minced garlic.

Ginger, commonly used as a seasoning in Japanese and Chinese cuisine, appears in a few recipes in this book. You can purchase fresh ginger at any well-stocked supermarket. It is normally carried in large, many-lobed roots. Break off a small-ish lobe and store it in a cool, dry place in the kitchen. When you are ready to use it, peel the root delicately with a paring knife and mince or grate it. A thick, juicy, aromatic pulp will result, which can be measured out. If the root dries up before you use it all, peel the shriveled root as well as you can and use your ginger grater to create a pungent fresh ginger powder. Store this in a dark, dry place and use it when a recipe calls for ground ginger.

Quantities of both garlic and ginger can be altered to suit your taste. In each recipe, we offer our recommendation as to what creates a well-balanced flavor, but your idea of well balanced may differ from ours. In all cases, with all seasonings, let your own experience and palate be your guide.

Herbs and Spices

A cupboard well stocked with herbs and spices is a treasure trove for every cook. An amazing number of woody shrubs provide flavorful roots, leaves, stems, seeds, and flowers that not only season a dish but bolster its content of vitamins and minerals.

Of particular interest to pasta cooks—certainly to those with Italian leanings—are basil, oregano, rosemary, parsley, bay leaves, and nutmeg. Flat-leaf parsley, often referred to as Italian parsley, has a more distinctive flavor than the curly-leaf type. Dried red chili flakes are used in many of our recipes. Tarragon also makes several appearances. When stocking your herb shelf, be sure to include at least these basics.

Many dishes with Mexican and Chinese flavors call for fresh cilantro (also known as fresh coriander or Chinese parsley). If you particularly enjoy these types of cuisine, keep fresh cilantro on hand.

Freshly ground black pepper enlivens many of our favorite dishes. Invest in a simple pepper grinder and keep a supply of peppercorns on hand. Commercially packaged ground black pepper just isn't the same. Curry powder is a favorite seasoning of those who enjoy spicy cuisine. Different brands can vary vastly in potency, so discover one that suits your taste. Use curry (and all spicy seasonings) with discretion when guests are coming to dinner. Cayenne, the fiery red pepper of curry fame, provides an extra punch in certain strongly flavored dishes. Again, exercise caution.

An herb garden is one of the most satisfying projects creative cooks can undertake. In pots or in a spot of ground near your back door, plant seeds or set out seedlings purchased from a local nursery. Most herbs are easy to grow and quite hardy, so you needn't tend them much. Adequate water and sunlight are the only essentials for healthy and abundant herb plants. Some leafy herbs, such as basil and cilantro, are annuals and must be replanted each year. Woodier varieties—rosemary and oregano, for instance—will establish themselves readily in the right spot and will flourish for many, many years. You can easily dry fresh herbs from the garden by hanging them in a dark, dry place for several days.

If you don't wish to grow them yourself, you can buy fresh herbs at delicatessens or the larger supermarkets. Dried herbs in tins and jars are available at every grocery, but we suggest you seek out a source of bulk dried herbs—many natural food stores carry them. Then you can buy in small quantities at very reasonable prices. How many times have you paid a pound or more for a fancy jar of spice, and never used more than a teaspoon or two? Store all dried herbs and spices covered in a dry, dark place to preserve freshness. Ground seasonings, in particular, lose their flavors rapidly.

In most dishes, you can use either fresh or dried herbs. Pesto is an obvious exception—only fresh herbs will work. As a general rule of thumb, use twice as much of a fresh herb as you would dried. If a recipe calls for 1 teaspoon dried oregano, for instance, you can use 2 teaspoons minced fresh oregano with good results.

Cheeses

We insist on natural cheeses, produced without added enzymes, gums, or preservatives. Become a label reader and select only real, pure cheese—avoid products labeled "processed" or "cheese food." Low-salt varieties may be easier on our blood pressure and are often just as flavorful as their salted counterparts. Many manufacturers are also offering skim-milk varieties. Some are quite tasty and can be substituted for their higher-fat counterparts in our recipes.

Dry, hard cheeses like Parmesan and Romano are high in fat and salt but impart a lot of flavor, even in small quantities. It's hard to imagine a pasta pantry without them. We buy these hard cheeses in wedges, grate them in sizable quantities, and store the grated cheese in the refrigerator in tightly closed containers (see Grinders and Graters on page 13). Parmesan, Romano, and Asiago can be used interchangeably in our recipes, with only slight variations in flavor.

Goat cheeses have a unique piquant flavor that some people adore; others find them too strong or "goaty." Feta, made from goat or sheep milk, must be stored in water in your refrigerator to retain its freshness. Other types of cheese should be tightly wrapped and stored in the refrigerator.

Mushrooms

Because mushrooms are succulent and rich in flavor, they play an important role in many types of cuisine. Pasta is no exception. Many varieties of mushroom are available to today's cook, so you can experiment almost endlessly.

The fresh button mushroom most familiar to Americans is versatile and delicious. Choose button mushrooms that are an even white or light brown in color, with caps tightly closed against the stem. Store fresh button mushrooms in a dry paper or linen bag in the salad drawer of your refrigerator. They will retain optimum flavor and texture for only a few days, so buy in small quantities.

For a few pounds you can buy a mushroom brush, which is the perfect implement for removing loose dirt particles without damaging the mushroom's tender flesh. Brush the dirt from the mushrooms and slice off the often tough tip of the stem. Use them whole, halved, quartered, or sliced.

Also commonly available in their fresh form are shiitake—the rich, black mushroom of the Asian chef—and oyster mushrooms. Sometimes one can also find fresh cepes, chanterelles, morels, and other field mushrooms. All these varieties offer distinctive flavors and textures. Of course, there are many varieties of poisonous—even lethal—mushrooms, so don't pick the fresh fungus you find in your garden and throw it into the pot! It takes an experienced person to safely identify edible mushrooms.

Dried mushrooms further expand the variety of mushroom textures and flavors. Dried shiitake can be purchased in every Asian market. They are softened by soaking in water and are then carefully washed before using. Porcini, astoundingly robust Italian field mushrooms, are also soaked to reconstitute them before being added to a dish. In either case, strain the soaking liquid through a few layers of cheesecloth or a paper coffee filter and use it if liquid is called for in the recipe, or as a soup stock the following day. Porcini liquid compares to beef stock in its richness.

Nuts and Seeds

Though nuts and seeds are high in fats—and therefore calories—they also provide amino acids, vitamins and minerals, and a great deal of flavor. Buy fresh, raw, unsalted nuts—in their shells when possible—and store in a cool, dry place. Once the shells are removed, the nuts should be stored in the refrigerator or freezer to avoid rancidity.

Seeds can also be purchased unsalted and raw—natural food stores often carry them in bulk. To protect their freshness, store seeds in tightly covered containers in a dark, dry cupboard or in the refrigerator.

Many of our recipes call for lightly toasted nuts or seeds. Toasting intensifies the natural flavors and imparts a pleasant subtle smokiness. (See page 20 for toasting instructions.)

Peanut butter and tahini (sesame paste) are examples of nut and seed preparations useful to the creative cook. Grind your own or purchase varieties that are made without additives and with little or no salt.

Beans

Beans are wonderfully nutritious, delicious, and economical. Combined with pasta, they create a protein- and fiber-rich meal substantial enough to satisfy any appetite. Buy dried beans in bulk at a natural food store for the best variety and quality. Store them in tightly closed containers in a dark, dry place.

Before cooking beans, rinse them thoroughly to remove surface dirt, and sort them carefully. Often small dirt clods, pebbles, and other foreign objects will find their way through the factory sorters and into the market bean bin.

Most beans must be soaked several hours to soften them before cooking (overnight is fine, or all day if you put them to soak first thing in the morning). Drain off the starchy soaking liquid, which contributes to indigestion in some people. Cover the beans with fresh, cold water and boil them until they're tender. You may wish to add garlic, bay leaves, and/or dried red chili flakes to the cooking water, but wait to salt the pot until the beans are tender and ready for their final seasoning, because cooking in salt can give the beans a tough or rubbery texture.

When beans are to be added to another dish, as with the recipes in this book, be sure you do not let them get too soft in the boiling pot. Ideally, the beans will have a firm but delicate texture, yielding easily to the bite but not mushy.

Tofu and Tempeh

Many vegetarians rely on tofu and tempeh, both derivatives of the soybean, as sources of concentrated protein. Tofu is made from soy milk curds and is available in a variety of textures, from silky smooth to coarse and firm. It tastes quite bland, and when added to pasta dishes will soak up the sauce and take on its flavor. Tofu can be sliced, diced, crumbled, or mashed. In every case, it is rinsed and blotted dry before using.

We often add tofu to ricotta cheese mixtures—in lasagna filling, for instance—because, when crumbled, its texture is similar. This increases the protein and calcium content of the dish and lowers the fat, without compromising the flavor.

Tempeh is a unique fermented soybean product with a chewy texture and authentic soybean flavor. It adds a hearty, even meaty, quality to certain dishes in this book.

Tofu and tempeh can be purchased at natural food stores and Asian specialty stores. In California, home to many health-conscious shoppers, tofu is available in the produce section of almost every supermarket. Tempeh, however, has yet to establish itself as a mainstream commodity. If you would like to be able to purchase tofu and tempeh at your local grocery, the manager may be willing to order it for you.

Fresh tofu keeps for a few days if stored in a bowl of water in the refrigerator. The water should be changed every day. You can also freeze tofu, though when frozen and thawed it takes on a spongy quality which will not lend itself to all tofu uses.

The refrigerator life of fresh tempeh is only a few days, so buy it just before you intend to use it, or freeze it if you wish to

stock up. Tempeh freezes and thaws with no noticeable altera-
tion in flavor or texture.

Tools of the Craft

Artisans in every field will tell you that good tools are absolutely essential to creating fine things. Owning dishes and
equipment of high quality will enhance your cooking experience considerably. There is great joy to be had in building
piece by piece a beautiful and efficient cookware collection,
whether at a gourmet kitchen shop or at flea markets and gar-
age sales.

In writing this book, we have assumed that you are cooking in a kitchen well equipped with the basics. We offer the following suggestions regarding tools particular to pasta cooking.
The essentials are few and simple.

Pasta Pot

Any large stockpot can be used as your pasta-boiling kettle. It
must hold a minimum of 6 quarts of water, and it should have a
tight-fitting lid, because a closed pot will boil much more
quickly than an open one. Since you will be using this vessel
over high heat, select one with a heavy bottom that will con-
duct heat evenly and will not warp over time. You may want to
purchase more than one, as such a pot will also be useful for
cooking soups and blanching tomatoes.

Colanders

The draining of pasta will soon become a frequent ritual, and
the colander a valued utensil. Easy cleanup makes stainless
steel colanders, which are sometimes coated with enamel,

preferable. Obtain both a small one for intimate family use and a large one for grand affairs. Buy colanders with handles on both sides, since you will want to pick up the colander and shake it for really thorough draining. The footed type is ideal, since it holds the draining pasta a few inches away from the sink for maximum efficiency. If you choose to reuse pasta cooking water in the garden (but only if it isn't salted; see page 299), place the colander over a large basin or kettle to collect the liquid as it drains off.

Pasta Machine

We have tried various types of pasta machines over the years, and keep coming back to the simplest: a heavy stainless steel, hand-cranked, countertop model that rolls the kneaded dough to the desired thickness and cuts it into uniform shapes. Though rolling pasta dough by hand and cutting it with a knife can work quite well, this device simplifies and expedites the process. The electric mix-and-extrude-type machine may work for you, but we prefer the more energy-efficient model for best hand-made results.

Pasta Servers

Two specialized implements are available for serving pasta. Simple salad tongs—the stainless steel variety hinged together at the base—allow for efficient one-handed serving while the other hand holds the plate. Alternately, many people use a specialized gadget called a pasta claw, available in plastic, wood, or stainless steel. The noodles wrap around its stiff fingers and are then carried to the plate. Or you can simply use two wooden spoons, or a wooden fork and spoon, to lift the pasta from serving vessel to plate. For soups, of course, a ladle is the ideal serving implement. Acquire one with a large cup. Tongs, wooden implements, or steel-spring spoons are all useful tools for serving salad.

Food Processor

There is certainly nothing absolutely essential about a food processor—unless you are a serious cook! The vast capabilities of
these devices open up new worlds of culinary possibility. For
certain jobs, like pesto making, cheese grating, or fine mincing
of ingredients, the time saved by a food processor is considerable. A blender can come in handy for some simple blending
jobs, but invest in a real food processor as soon as you can.
Today, small-capacity machines are available, which can serve
most purposes for a fraction of the cost of the larger models.

Grinders and Graters

Canned ground spices bear very little resemblance to the
aromatic powder that results when you grind whole spices as
you need them. Noteworthy examples are black pepper,
cloves, nutmeg, and mustard. You may wish to purchase a
small electric coffee grinder to use only for spices (be sure to
label it prominently so some unintiated soul doesn't use it for
coffee!). For similar results, you can obtain a mortar and pestle—a sharply ridged bowl with pounding stick—and engage
in the ancient cooking ritual of manually breaking up spices to
release their flavors. Specialized grinders are available for
black pepper and whole nutmeg. They are worth the invest-
ment. Spices and herbs are the cook's inspiration—make the
most of them by preparing them fresh.

    Graters come in a wide variety of shapes and sizes. The
standard flat grater or the four-sided stand-up model are both
quite adequate for most tasks. We both own tripod hand-crank
disc graters and rely on them for large grating jobs. These wonderful little machines come with different sizes of grating and
slicing discs, and yours will soon become indispensable. For
grating hard cheeses like Parmesan, a food processor will save
you time and effort.

Perfect Pasta
Every Time

Selecting the Noodle

Fresh pasta or dried? What a happy choice! Either way, you
can dazzle family and friends with your delicious sauce in-
ventions.

Some cooks have a strong preference for fresh pasta.
Newly made noodles can have a delightfully delicate texture
and a bright, fresh taste. Also, consider the simple pleasure to
be had in preparing food from scratch. If you enjoy being indus-

trious in your kitchen, creating fresh pasta may become a favorite pastime. There is an art to pasta-making. If the dough is kneaded too little or too much, you may end up with pasta that is rubbery or limp. Attention to the task can avert these disasters, however, so please don't hesitate to give it a try.

At fine gourmet food stores, commercially prepared fresh noodles come in a variety of herb and vegetable flavors not commonly available dried. Be aware of dates on the packaging, though. Fresh pasta that sits too long at the market develops an off flavor that no sauce, however inspired, can mask. Select fresh noodles that are no more than a day (perhaps two) old.

Some cooks greatly prefer dried pasta, not only for its convenience but because the hard semolina wheat used by most commercial pasta manufacturers ensures real body to the pasta (so long as it's not overcooked!). We find that dried semolina pasta is delicious for most purposes. Locate an Italian delicatessen in your community for the largest selection of shapes and sizes.

Many of our recipes suggest using Asian noodle varieties. Many well-stocked supermarkets sell fresh Chinese noodles and wonton wrappers, which are delicious. You might be able to seek out buckwheat, rice, or yam flours to make your own Asian noodles from scratch, but we find the dried noodles sold in great variety at specialty food markets to be quite fine.

Couscous is a pasta import from North Africa. The tiny beads of dried flour and water cook almost instantly, creating a light and fluffy texture perfect for salads and casseroles. Couscous is available at any well-stocked supermarket.

In summary, with so many good dried and fresh noodles available in Italian and Asian food stores—and even standard supermarkets—there's no need to invest the time required to make your own. But it's fun now and then to begin at the beginning if you have plenty of time and want to experience the joys of "from scratch" cooking. The recipes in this book are written primarily for dried noodles, but you may substitute the fresh variety. One pound dried pasta is equivalent to 1½ pounds fresh, so convert the recommended amounts and you will be sure to prepare enough.

With this in mind, we provide here a basic and relatively simple egg pasta recipe. In addition to the right ingredients, all you need is a large work surface, a rolling pin, and a knife or scissors for cutting the shapes. If you find you love it and want to enjoy fresh pasta more than occasionally, consider investing in a hand-crank pasta machine, which will roll the dough out to a uniform thickness and will cut strands of varying widths quickly and easily.

Basic Egg Noodles

Yield: 1½ pounds (enough for about 4 servings)

White plain flour	1¾	cup
Semolina flour	½	cup
Salt	½	teaspoon
Eggs	3	large, room temperature
Olive oil	1	tablespoon
Water	3	tablespoons

Place flours and salt in the work bowl of a food processor and process briefly to combine. With machine running, add eggs, oil, and water and process until dough resembles coarse cornmeal and sticks together when pressed between thumb and forefinger. If you don't own a food processor, stir together the flours and salt and pour into a compact mound on your work surface. Make a well in the center of the mound and pour in the slightly beaten eggs, oil, and water. Stir with a fork, incorporating the flour a little at a time, until you have a smooth dough.

Wrap the dough in a floured tea towel and set aside at room temperature for about 30 minutes. Knead gently about 10 times, then roll out with a rolling pin to desired thickness and cut into shapes. You may also use a hand-crank pasta machine for these steps, following manufacturer's directions. If preparing in advance, spread pasta out on a floured tea towel, dust with a little flour, and toss occasionally until you are ready for it. Pasta can also be left to dry on the towel, or on a rack, for longer periods. When it is completely dry, store it in a sealed container in a dark, dry place until needed.

Variations: A lovely green pasta will result if you substitute ¼ pound fresh pureed spinach for one of the eggs. For herb-flecked pasta, add ¼ cup minced fresh basil or ½ cup minced fresh tarragon to the flour mixture. Wonderful pasta can be made using minced dried tomatoes or chilies, or any number of other ingredients. Experiment and see what flavor discoveries you can make on your own.

Each serving provides:

339	Calories	53 g	Carbohydrate
12 g	Protein	322 mg	Sodium
8 g	Fat	159 mg	Cholesterol

Perfecting the Noodle

"He can't even boil water!" So complained a close friend about her kitchen-phobic husband. Well, he might have trouble becoming a pasta chef. But anyone who's mastered the boiling of water can easily learn to delight family and friends with delicious pasta.

A great pasta dinner depends on a well-cooked noodle, so the boiling part is important. To begin with, use plenty of water: 3–4 quarts per pound of pasta is about right. Bring it to a real rolling boil (a lid on the pot helps this happen faster) before adding a bit of olive oil and a shake or two of salt. Those with fat- or salt-related health concerns can skip these ingredients, but they are part of the time-tested method for a successful batch of noodles.

Add the pasta all at once to the boiling water, separating the strands a little as you immerse them. Now, stay close to the pot! Stir the noodles regularly to see that they aren't sticking together or to the pan. If you are still in the middle of preparing the sauce or some other part of the meal, set a timer to alert you when the pasta cooking time is almost up. If you are using store-bought dried noodles, the package will give you the approximate cooking time. Set your timer for just a couple of minutes less than is recommended so you can pull out a noodle and bite into it to test for doneness.

Most pasta chefs prefer their noodles cooked to the "al dente" stage. This Italian phrase means "to the tooth" and suggests that the tooth should meet a little resistance in the pasta. Undercooked pasta has a tough center and an unpleasant starchy taste. Cooked too long, noodles break apart easily and turn to mush in the mouth. You must learn to get it right! If you are calmly attentive the first few times you try, soon it will become second nature to recognize perfectly cooked noodles.

Fresh noodles, whether homemade or store-bought, cook very rapidly—in only a minute or two, depending on their shape and texture. When cooking fresh pasta, don't leave the pot even for a moment! Stir the noodles in, watch as the water comes back to a boil, then immediately pull out a noodle and bite into it. If it's not yet al dente it soon will be, so stay and check again half a minute or so later.

We would recommend one exception to the al dente rule: Some Asian noodles, particularly soba (made with buckwheat flour) and rice flour noodles, taste better if they are cooked to the soft stage. Not mushy, but a bit beyond al dente.

When the pasta is cooked to perfection, drain it quickly in a large colander, allowing just a little water to cling to each noodle (unless a recipe stipulates thorough draining). Toss the pasta and sauce together in a serving dish. A warmed platter or bowl is preferable, as most pasta dishes are at their best served really hot. A serving bowl can be warmed briefly atop your boiling pasta pot, or use the oven or a warm spot on your stovetop.

It works best to have the sauce ready when the noodles come out of the pot, but timing is not always perfect. If you must hold the noodles for a few minutes, toss them with a little butter or olive oil in the still warm but dry boiling pot and keep a lid on until you're ready for them. Or, if you know ahead of time that the sauce is going to take a bit longer, stop the pasta water from boiling and let the noodles simply rest in the hot water while the sauce catches up. But pay attention! Though it cooks more slowly once the burner is turned off, the pasta will get overly soft if left in the water too long. This method is for the rare emergency when the sauce is running only a few minutes behind.

There may come a time when you will need to hold the cooked, unsauced pasta a long while before serving. Or you may have leftover plain pasta to heat up. When this happens, boil a pot of water and stir the noodles in for about 30 seconds just before tossing with the sauce. If a finished pasta gets gooey from sitting too long before serving, incorporate hot water a drizzle at a time to correct the consistency.

If you're making pasta salad, cool the noodles by plunging them into a bowl of cold water for 2 to 3 minutes (this is preferable to the running-faucet cooling method because it conserves water). If your salad dressing isn't ready yet, toss the noodles with a little olive oil and set aside in the refrigerator.

Some people like a greater ratio of sauce to noodle; adjust the recommended amount of pasta to suit your taste. Learn to trust yourself more than even the most famous cookbook authors.

Pasta cooking can be a wonderfully relaxing and creative experience. The basics are easy to learn. Use high-quality ingredients, and have fun in the kitchen!

The Basics of Sauce

As we have said elsewhere, the fun of cooking is in experimentation. This makes pasta one of the cook's most enjoyable foods, because the possibilities for sauce are practically limitless. Within each category, we provide numerous examples of how we combine our favorite foods with pasta. We invite you to take off from there.

In an introduction to each recipe section, we have provided tips and techniques for successful sauce preparation. Please read those introductions for a comprehensive overview.

Here, we explain some basic flavor-enhancing techniques used in various recipes in this book. They are simple and quick procedures. Once you have mastered them, you will find them quite useful.

Toasting Seeds and Nuts

Place nuts or seeds in a single layer in a heavy-bottomed skillet over medium-high heat on the stovetop. Shake the pan frequently and soon the nuts or seeds will be golden brown and will emit a wonderful roasted aroma. Whole spices, like mustard or cumin seeds, are done when they begin to pop vigorously in the pan. Remove immediately from the pan and set aside until needed.

Blanching and Seeding Tomatoes

Bring several quarts of water to a boil in a large lidded pot (the same water can be used later for cooking pasta). Drop in the fresh tomatoes. Within a minute or two, their skins will begin to split and pull away from the flesh. Remove with a slotted spoon to a bowl of cold water. When they are cool enough to handle, remove the skins of the tomatoes and cut out the stems. If you are using pear tomatoes (also known as plum tomatoes), they can be coarsely chopped and used without further preparation. If using the rounder salad type, cut the peeled tomatoes in half crosswise and gently squeeze to remove the juicy seed pockets. Now chop the tomatoes coarsely and proceed with the recipe.

Roasting Vegetables

Certain vegetables take on a delightful smoky flavor when roasted. Peppers and small aubergines lend themselves most readily to this type of preparation. Place the vegetable under a very hot grill and turn every few minutes until the entire surface is charred black. Remove it to a paper or plastic bag, close, and set aside for about 15 minutes. The steam in the bag will finish the cooking and the vegetable will become quite soft. When cool enough to handle, remove it from the bag and peel off the charred skin. Remove stems and/or seeds and chop or mash before proceeding with the recipe.

Nutrition Alert

People who are concerned about nutrition balance their food intake based on factors beyond the outmoded "five basic food groups" concept. Some of us do this because of a health condition that requires special attention; others simply want to maintain the best health possible.

Many studies have been conducted to determine optimum levels of various food components in the human diet. Our intent here is to suggest some guidelines based on the latest findings. For further investigation, check with your local librarian or bookseller.

Each recipe in this book has been analyzed for calories, fats, proteins, carbohydrates, cholesterol, and sodium.

Calories. Almost everyone is concerned about calories—either with ingesting too many or, rarely, too few. It is important to be aware of your total caloric intake in a day, but most important to note is where the calories are coming from. Calories derive from three primary sources: proteins, carbohydrates, and fats. Fats contain a greater concentration of calories than do carbohydrates or protein, and they are much harder for the body to metabolize. Government dietary experts suggest that the average British diet be adjusted so that fewer calories come from fatty foods and more from carbohydrates. Pasta fits nicely into this picture, providing a good carbohydrate foundation for a meal.

Fats. In the nutritional analyses provided here, fat is listed in grams per serving. A gram of fat has 9 calories, and the average tablespoon of oil contains 125 calories. To help you put this in perspective, consider that a tablespoon of sugar contains 54 calories. Calories derived from dietary fats are more troublesome than calories from any other source, as the body is most efficient at converting fat calories into body fat. The British Heart Foundation recommends limiting fat intake to no more than 40 percent of total energy intake.

Although sophisticated nutritional studies have broken fats into three classifications—saturated, monounsaturated, and polyunsaturated—the recipes in this book have been analyzed for overall fat content, to offer a basic guideline for monitoring dietary fat intake.

Proteins. Protein is also analyzed in this book for grams per serving. Each gram of protein contains only 4 calories. Since our bodies store only small amounts of protein, it needs to be replenished on a daily basis. Most people associate protein consumption with eating animal products; however, protein in our recipes derives from combining grains (pasta flour) with soy products, dairy products, beans, and nuts. Readers who are not vegetarians may wish to serve a pasta dish as an accompaniment to meat or fish, keeping overall protein (and fat) intake in mind. Recent nutritional studies suggest that the detrimental effects of excessive protein consumption should be of greater concern to most British people than the threat of protein deficiency.

Carbohydrates. Carbohydrates are analyzed here for grams per serving. Each carbohydrate gram provides 4 calories, equivalent to proteins. Carbohydrates such as pasta, grains, and potatoes were once thought to be high in calories and low in nutritive value. However, nutritional experts now suggest that more of our daily calories come from carbohydrates and fewer from protein, since the body derives energy more "economically" from carbohydrates.

Cholesterol. Cholesterol content is listed in milligrams for our recipes. Many volumes have been written on this subject in recent years, and much is being discovered about its role in overall health and nutrition. Accumulation of cholesterol in the cells lining our artery walls can lead to atherosclerosis, heart attacks, and strokes. More crucial to the health of your blood vessels than cholesterol count, however, is the amount of total dietary fats you ingest.

Sodium. Sodium content of our recipes is listed in milligrams. The British Heart Foundation recommends that sodium intake be limited to 5,000 milligrams a day (a teaspoon of salt contains 2,300 milligrams of sodium). High sodium intake is associated with high blood pressure and such life-threatening conditions as heart and kidney diseases and strokes. Many foods naturally contain some sodium, so you do not need to add much when cooking to achieve good flavors. Particularly if you have salt-related health concerns, dishes that taste a little bland unsalted can be seasoned with herbs or other salt-free alternatives. Where our recipes do call for salt, you may add less than the recommended amount or none at all, if you wish.

Monitoring your intake of these food components is important; however, unless under doctor's instructions, you needn't be overly rigid. It is acceptable to balance your intake over the course of a day, rather than attempting to make each meal fit the pattern recommended by nutritional experts. This rule of thumb allows you to enjoy a recipe that may be higher in fat or salt, for instance, than you would normally choose, knowing that at your next meal you can eliminate that component altogether to achieve a healthy daily balance.

The information given here is not set in stone; the science of nutrition is constantly evolving. We encourage you to spend some time learning about how foods break down and are used by the body as fuel. A basic understanding of the process and application of a few simple rules can contribute to a longer and—more important—healthier life.

An Introduction to the Recipes

Before you try our recipes, we want to outline some basic information that we hope will make using them an experience of great pleasure.

There are a few standard rules for preparing to cook from a recipe.

1. Use only the freshest, best-quality ingredients. Your finished dish will be only as good as the individual components that go into it, so don't compromise on quality. (We've said this before, but it bears repeating.)

2. Read the recipe all the way through before beginning. This will give you a solid understanding of the entire process so you can proceed with confidence. You wouldn't think of building a house without first having studied the blueprints!

3. Set all of your ingredients out on the work surface before you begin. This will save you walking from one end of the kitchen to the other to rummage in a cupboard for the long-lost paprika, while your vegetables are overcooking on the stove.

4. For certain ingredients, quantities are by nature somewhat approximate. When we call for a large carrot, for instance, the one you use may be more or less large than ours. This is nothing to worry about. When it is essential to the success of a dish to use a very specific amount, we will provide cup or pound measurements. Otherwise, use your own judgment in deciding which carrot is "large." Our method with garlic deserves special mention here. We have listed garlic amounts in "medium" cloves. If you are using elephant garlic, or the tiny new cloves at the center of a garlic bulb, adjust accordingly the number of cloves you use.

5. Seasonings are a matter of personal taste. Naturally, we have provided recipes for dishes that taste good to us, seasoned as we like them. Certain people will prefer more or less of certain seasonings: salt and garlic are prominent examples. Of course, you may do as you please. We often customize favorite recipes from cookbooks, and we encourage you to do the same.

6. When serving hot food, use warmed serving dishes and warmed plates so the food stays at optimum temperature as long as possible. This is easily accomplished by placing the dishes near the heat source as you cook; or warm your oven several minutes before dinnertime, turn off the heat, and place your dishes there until needed.

You will notice that our recipes list ingredients in an unconventional format: name of food in first column, quantity required in a separate column to the right. This allows the quickest perusal of the ingredients, so you can determine whether you're in the mood for that particular dish, and whether you have the required foods on hand. We find this format particularly easy to follow, and hope you will agree.

Some recipes in this book carry an "Almost Instant" designation. This means that you can prepare the sauce in the time it takes to boil water and cook the pasta. When time is short, check for "Almost Instant" dishes in the recipe lists under chapter headings in the table of contents. Put the pasta water on and you're almost there!

Now, we invite you to enjoy our favorite pasta dishes.

Pestos

The word *pesto* literally means "paste." The fresh basil version is an Italian classic and now a common British restaurant and supermarket offering; many other foods lend themselves to this type of preparation as well. Once you are accustomed to the basic technique, experiment and enjoy!

The classic pesto ingredients are fresh herbs, nuts, cheese, and garlic—with an emphasis on the garlic. For many, in fact, eating pesto is a fine way to achieve garlic bliss. Some of the recipes in this section suggest using just a clove or two so the more subtle flavors aren't lost. You may use whatever amount of garlic suits your taste, of course.

A revelation of freshness, most pesto is uncooked and quick to prepare. Once the raw ingredients are readied for blending, you're only a few minutes away from serving time. Before the age of electricity, cooks used a mortar and pestle to pound their ingredients into a thick mush. Today, a food processor saves a great deal of time and effort. A blender can also do the job, though not as efficiently.

High-quality ingredients are essential to great pesto. Make sure greens and herbs are crisply fresh, and dry them well before blending (a salad spinner works well for this). You want a finished product that is wonderfully thick, not watery. Shell the nuts immediately before using (except in the case of pine nuts, which are difficult to find in their natural state). Nuts sold already shelled are often rancid in the package and will ruin your pesto. Use the finest-quality cheeses and the best olive oil—extra virgin—because its authentic olive flavor pulls the other tastes together.

Pesto improves over time as the flavors blend. For this reason, we prefer preparing pesto ahead of time and storing it, covered, in the refrigerator at least several hours before using. The basic herbal pestos will keep in the refrigerator several weeks, while the more exotic pestos should be used within a few days. Many pestos can also be made in large quantities and frozen in small jars until needed. But don't try it with those that contain high-water-content dairy products (sour cream, for instance). These milk products may separate when thawed and ruin the consistency of your pesto. Hard, dry cheeses like Parmesan are an exception to this rule.

If you are using pesto that has been frozen or refrigerated, bring it to room temperature before using it. A cold pesto will cool your noodles too rapidly. Also, the cooked pasta should be really hot when you add the pesto, so the thick sauce will be liquefied a bit and will coat the noodles well.

Don't overlook the many other uses for pesto. We enjoy it as a sandwich or cracker spread, either plain or in combination with cream cheese. It can also be used in soups, salad dressings, and as a stuffing seasoning.

Pasta al pesto is at once simple and sophisticated. If you are not yet a devoted pesto lover, the following recipes will make one of you.

Basic Herbal Pestos

Your favorite herbs can be easily transformed into flavorful pastes for pasta saucing, and other uses. The basic herbal pastes discussed here are called for as flavoring agents in a number of recipes throughout this book. Grow your own herbs, if you can, and stock up on a variety of pestos. You will discover many creative ways to enjoy them.

To whip up a quick and delicious meal, heat several quarts of water and boil pasta until al dente. Drain and toss with enough pesto to coat the noodles well. (As a rule of thumb, use 1 cup pesto for 1 pound pasta.) Add additional cheese if desired.

The strong, woody flavors of rosemary and oregano may not appeal in concentrated form to all palates, so experiment to see what you like.

Classic Basil Pesto

We have both prepared this simple version of the classic Genovese pesto for years, using aromatic basil picked fresh from the summer garden. It is satisfying work which will bring you and your friends great pleasure at the table.

Yield: 1 cup

Fresh basil leaves	**2**	**cups, firmly packed**
Olive oil	**⅓**	**cup**
Pine nuts	**¼**	**cup**
Garlic	**6**	**medium cloves, chopped**
Parmesan cheese, finely grated	**¾**	**cup**

Wash the basil, discard the stems, and spin dry. In a food processor or blender puree basil with ¼ cup of the olive oil, the pine nuts, garlic, and Parmesan until thick and homogenous. With the machine running, add the remaining olive oil in a thin stream to form a smooth paste.

Note: If you are harvesting basil from the garden at season's end, a few simple tips will facilitate cleaning of the leaves. Use your clippers to snip off the main stems near the base of the plant, rather than pulling them up by the roots. Put a spray attachment on your hose and wash down the plants before bringing them into the kitchen.

Each serving (1 tablespoon) provides:

85	Calories	4 g	Carbohydrate
3 g	Protein	87 mg	Sodium
7 g	Fat	4 mg	Cholesterol

Rosemary Pesto

Rosemary is a strong-flavored herb that makes an exciting and unusual pesto. A flat-leaf variety can be grown in home gardens. It is more fragrant and finer in texture than the more common woody type. Either will work, but remember, a little goes a long way. To create a sauce for 8 ounces of noodles, whip ⅓ cup pesto with about ¼ cup half-and-half or light sour cream. Toss with hot pasta and enjoy.

Yield: 1 cup

Fresh parsley	1½	cups, firmly packed
Fresh rosemary leaves	½	cup, loosely packed
Garlic	6	medium cloves, chopped
Olive oil	½	cup
Parmesan cheese, finely grated	½	cup
Dried red chili flakes	¼	teaspoon
Raw walnuts, chopped	¼	cup

Wash the parsley and rosemary, discard stems, and spin dry. In a food processor or blender puree herbs, garlic, and ¼ cup of the olive oil until thick and homogenous. Add the Parmesan, chili flakes, and walnuts, and blend again. With the machine running, add the remaining olive oil in a thin stream. A thick, rich paste will result.

Each serving (1 tablespoon) provides:

93	Calories	2 g	Carbohydrate
2 g	Protein	60 mg	Sodium
9 g	Fat	2 mg	Cholesterol

Cilantro Pesto

Of course, you must be a cilantro fan to enjoy the flavor of this pesto.
We love it simply spread on crackers with cream cheese. Or use it to
season Mexican pasta dishes, such as Pasta with Cilantro Pesto and
Avocado, page 135. The roasted garlic called for in this recipe
imparts a mellower, sweeter flavor than raw minced garlic.

Yield: 1½ cups

Garlic	1	large bulb
Pumpkin seeds	⅓	cup
Fresh cilantro	1	cup, firmly packed
Fresh parsley	1	cup, firmly packed
Olive oil	⅓	cup
Mild chili powder	2	teaspoons
Dried red chili flakes	1	teaspoon
Ground cumin	1	teaspoon
Lemon juice	¼	cup

Preheat oven or toaster oven to 350 degrees. Cut ¼ inch off the
garlic bulb to barely expose the tops of the cloves. Do not peel.
Drizzle on about ½ teaspoon olive oil and bake about 30–45
minutes. Alternately, bake in a microwave oven until soft,
about 15 minutes. When the garlic bulb is very soft, remove it
from the oven and cool. Remove the garlic from the skin by
squeezing the cloves from the bottom. The garlic will slide out
of the cut end as a soft paste. Toast the pumpkin seeds (see page
20).

Wash the cilantro and parsley, discard stems, and spin dry. In a food processor or blender, combine the cilantro, parsley, and olive oil. Puree into a thick paste. Add the garlic, toasted pumpkin seeds, chili powder, chili flakes, cumin, and lemon juice. Puree until smooth.

Each serving (1 tablespoon) provides:

38	Calories	2 g	Carbohydrate
0 g	Protein	5 mg	Sodium
3 g	Fat	0 mg	Cholesterol

Oregano Pesto

Oregano pesto is more delicate in flavor than many other herbal pestos. The herb is a perennial, so grow it in a large pot or on a small spot of unused ground to harvest year-round.

Yield: 1 cup

Fresh parsley	1½	cups, firmly packed
Fresh oregano leaves	½	cup, firmly packed
Olive oil	½	cup
Pine nuts	¼	cup
Garlic	4	medium cloves, chopped
Parmesan cheese, finely grated	½	cup
Port	2	teaspoons

Wash the parsley and oregano, discard stems, and spin dry. Combine parsley, oregano, and ¼ cup of the olive oil in a food processor or blender. Process briefly to chop the herbs. Add the pine nuts, garlic, and Parmesan. With the machine running, add the remaining oil in a thin stream, and the port. Process into a smooth paste.

Each serving (1 tablespoon) provides:

94	Calories	2 g	Carbohydrate
2 g	Protein	60 mg	Sodium
9 g	Fat	2 mg	Cholesterol

The Best 125 Meatless Pasta Dishes

Pesto Exotica

Many foods are perfect fodder for pesto. Your favorite combinations of flavors can easily be translated into delicious thick paste concoctions for pasta. Below are some of the near-infinite possibilities.

We include the amount of dried pasta recommended for a full recipe of pesto, as well as the number of servings provided by these amounts. We hope this will suggest to you that pesto is wonderful dinner party fare. If you are serving fewer people, simply reduce the amount of pasta accordingly and save the pesto that isn't used for another time. As a rule of thumb for moderate appetites, plan on 2 ounces of pasta per person for pesto side-dish servings and 3 ounces per person for pesto main-course servings.

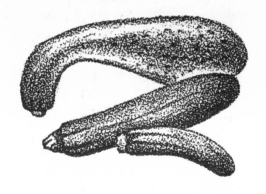

Pimiento Olive Pesto

The sharp flavor of pimiento-stuffed olives is mellowed here by the other ingredients. In fact, most people will not guess the primary ingredient of this pesto, though they will eat it in large quantities.

Yield: 8 main-course servings

Pimiento-stuffed olives, drained	1	cup
Raw walnuts, chopped	½	cup
Olive oil	¼	cup
Madeira	¼	cup
Parmesan cheese, finely grated	¼	cup
Fresh parsley, chopped	¼	cup, firmly packed
Garlic	2	medium cloves, chopped
Pepper		Several grinds
Dried pasta	1½	pounds

Recommended pasta: lasagnette or linguine

Puree all ingredients except pasta in a food processor or blender until a thick, color-flecked paste is formed. Prepare this pesto well ahead of time, if possible, so the flavors have time to blend. Store covered in the refrigerator. When ready to eat, put several quarts of water on to boil and bring the pesto to room temperature. Cook pasta in boiling water until al dente.

Toss the pesto with hot noodles in a warm bowl until well distributed. Pass more cheese and the pepper grinder, if you wish.

Each serving provides:			
471	Calories	67 g	Carbohydrate
14 g	Protein	473 mg	Sodium
16 g	Fat	2 mg	Cholesterol

Black Olive and Tomato Pesto

This tantalizing pesto is a quickie to prepare. The calamata or Greek olives add special pizzazz. A tart salad or a platter of crisp, raw bell pepper strips and garlic bread would be most welcome on the side.

Yield: 8 main-course servings

Pitted black olives, drained	1½ cups
Calamata or Greek olives, chopped	¼ cup, firmly packed
Olive oil	2 tablespoons
Tomato paste	⅓ cup
Dried oregano	1 teaspoon
Garlic	4 medium cloves, minced
Pepper	A few grinds
Parmesan cheese, finely grated	⅔ cup
Dried pasta	1½ pounds

Recommended pasta: vermicelli or linguine

Put several quarts of water on to boil for the pasta. Drain the olives and puree them with the oil, tomato paste, oregano, garlic, pepper, and ⅓ cup of the Parmesan in a food processor or blender to a thick, homogenous paste consistency. Cook the pasta until al dente and drain well. Toss in a warm bowl with the pesto. Serve immediately, passing additional Parmesan.

Each serving provides:

127	Calories	5 g	Carbohydrate
4 g	Protein	642 mg	Sodium
11 g	Fat	6 mg	Cholesterol

Roasted Red Bell Pepper Pesto

This makes a beautiful pale pink pesto which is lovely on a green noodle. Either home-roasted (see page 21) or commercially prepared peppers will do for this dish.

Yield: 8 main-course servings

Roasted red bell peppers	1	cup, loosely packed
Part-skim ricotta cheese	½	cup
Olive oil	¼	cup
Capers, drained	2	tablespoons
Garlic	2	medium cloves, chopped
Dried red chili flakes	¼	teaspoon
Salt		A scant pinch
Dried pasta	1½	pounds

Recommended pasta: spinach linguine or fettuccine

Several hours before dinnertime, puree all ingredients except the pasta in a food processor or blender to a thick, homogenous consistency. Store covered in the refrigerator. When ready to eat, put several quarts of water on to boil and bring the pesto to room temperature. Cook the pasta until al dente. Toss the pesto with hot pasta in a warm bowl until well distributed. Garnish with finely chopped fresh basil or parsley, if desired.

Each serving provides:

402	Calories	65 g	Carbohydrate
13 g	Protein	118 mg	Sodium
9 g	Fat	5 mg	Cholesterol

Spinach and Cheese Pesto with Pimiento

The red and green of this dish make it fun to serve around the holiday season; however, you will enjoy it any time of the year.

Yield: 4 main-course servings

Fresh spinach	2	pounds (or 1 10-ounce package frozen)
Plain lowfat yogurt	½	cup
Lowfat cottage cheese	⅔	cup
Freshly grated nutmeg	½	teaspoon
Garlic	2	medium cloves, minced
Olive oil	4	tablespoons
Pimiento, chopped	1	4-ounce jar, drained
Romano cheese, finely grated	⅓	cup
Dried pasta	12	ounces

Recommended pasta: linguine or sphaghetti

Put several quarts of water on to boil for the pasta. If using fresh spinach, carefully wash it, discard the stems, and place the leaves in a steamer rack over a couple of inches of boiling water in a lidded pot. Steam spinach until it wilts. Cool the cooked spinach in a colander, then squeeze out the excess water. (Alternately, thaw the frozen variety and squeeze out the excess water.) The spinach, whether fresh or frozen, must be as dry as possible. Using a food processor, blend the yogurt, cottage cheese, and nutmeg until smooth. Add the spinach, garlic, and 2 tablespoons of the oil and process until just incorporated. Use a double boiler to heat this mixture or place in a pan and cook gently over very low heat, stirring frequently, until heated through. Stir in the pimiento. Meanwhile, cook the pasta until al dente. Drain well and toss with remaining 2 tablespoons oil in a warm bowl. Toss with the pesto until well distributed and serve immediately. Pass Romano at the table and the pepper grinder, if you wish.

<hr>

Each serving provides:

553	Calories	75 g	Carbohydrate
24 g	Protein	395 mg	Sodium
18 g	Fat	10 mg	Cholesterol

<hr>

Shiitake and Spinach Pesto with Ginger

This dish never fails to surprise and delight our friends. The subtle flavor of spinach is enlivened by robust mushrooms, tangy ginger, and rich roasted sesame oil. A delicious journey to the East.

Yield: 8 main-course servings

Dried shiitake mushrooms	1	ounce
Fresh spinach	1	bunch (about ¾ pound)
Water chestnuts, chopped	⅓	cup
Fresh ginger, grated	2	tablespoons
Roasted sesame oil	2	tablespoons
Soy sauce	2	teaspoons
Garlic	2	medium cloves, chopped
Eggs	3	large, hard-boiled, finely chopped
Sesame seeds	2	tablespoons
Green onions	4	minced
Lemon wedges	1	per serving
Dried pasta	1½	pounds

Recommended pasta: Asian noodle of your choice (for example, soba or lo mein)

Soak mushrooms in 2 cups hot water an hour or two. Lift them out, reserving soaking water, and wash carefully under a thin stream of running water to remove all grit. Squeeze liquid out of mushrooms and remove the tough stems. Strain mushroom soaking liquid through a paper coffee filter and set aside. Meanwhile, carefully wash the spinach, discard the stems, and place the leaves in a steamer rack over a couple of inches of boiling water in a lidded pot. Steam until it wilts. This may need to be done in several batches, depending on the size of your steamer. When cool, use your hands to squeeze out all liquid. Chop the spinach coarsely. Combine softened mushrooms, cooked spinach, ½ cup mushroom soaking liquid, the water chestnuts, ginger, sesame oil, soy sauce, and garlic in a food processor and puree until thick and smooth. This can be done several hours in advance. Set the pesto aside in the refrigerator, where the flavors will blend.

When ready to eat, bring several quarts of water to a boil and bring the pesto to room temperature. Toast the sesame seeds (see page 20). Cook the pasta until al dente. Drain well. Toss hot noodles with pesto in a warm bowl and sprinkle generously with eggs, sesame seeds, and green onions. Serve at once with lemon wedges.

Each serving provides:

420	Calories	72 g	Carbohydrate
16 g	Protein	152 mg	Sodium
8 g	Fat	80 mg	Cholesterol

Dried-Tomato Pesto with Mint

The almost smoky richness of dried tomatoes combines well with the bright flavors of fresh mint and feta cheese.

Yield: 10 main-course servings

Oil-packed dried tomatoes	¾ cup, loosely packed
Fresh mint leaves	½ cup, firmly packed
Raw walnuts, chopped	½ cup
Tomato paste	⅓ cup
Olive oil	¼ cup
Garlic	2 medium cloves, chopped
Salt	A scant pinch
Pepper	Several grinds
Feta cheese	½ pound
Lemon wedges	1 per serving
Dried pasta	2 pounds

Recommended pasta: **sturdy tubes or spirals**

Drain as much oil as possible from tomatoes before measuring. Well ahead of serving time (up to several days), puree the tomatoes, mint, walnuts, tomato paste, olive oil, garlic, salt, and pepper. Do not expect a smooth consistency. Store covered in the refrigerator. When ready to eat, put several quarts of water on to boil and bring the pesto to room temperature. Cook the pasta until al dente. Drain well. Toss in a warm bowl with the pesto and the crumbled feta cheese. Serve with lemon wedges and pass the pepper grinder.

Each serving provides:

540	Calories	79 g	Carbohydrate
17 g	Protein	348 mg	Sodium
18 g	Fat	20 mg	Cholesterol

Soups with Pasta

Soup is an age-old comfort food. By its very nature it is among the most wholesome of cooked fare—well-saturated ingredients are easy to digest, and the broth collects all the nutrients that can be lost during other types of cooking.

Whether simple and refreshing or complex and hearty, pasta soups are particularly satisfying. Except perhaps at their lightest, they can stand alone as a meal in a bowl—with bread and a tart, leafy salad rounding things out.

The savor of some soups depends on good stock. When you practice the art of making fresh stock, you participate in a timeless international tradition. Many dedicated cooks collect and refrigerate clean vegetable parings for a few days—including the skins of well-scrubbed potatoes. These are combined in fresh water and simmered gently an hour or so to yield, when strained, a tasty and delicate broth which is a fine soup base. When you steam vegetables, save the steaming water to add to your stock.

Wherever the recipes in this chapter call for water, this type of homemade stock can be used with delicious results. Of course, different combinations of vegetables will create distinctly different stocks. Experiment and discover your favorite intermingling of flavors for various soups.

If you haven't the time or inclination to make your own vegetable stock, convenient broth enhancers are available. Many of the recipes in this section use the following preparations:

- *Miso* is a nutritious savory soybean paste that is added to hot soup just before serving (about 1 tablespoon miso to 1 quart soup). Whisk it with a few tablespoons of water, then stir thoroughly into the pot. The miso is suspended in the soup in a lovely light cloud.

- *Vegetable broth cubes* produce a light and savory broth. In some of our recipes, we use a "no salt added" vegetable broth cube. One 0.35-ounce (10 gram) cube contains only 213 mg sodium and makes three 6-ounce servings of broth. The brand we use is imported from Switzerland and is available at health food stores, some large supermarket chains, and imported food outlets. If you can't locate a low-sodium vegetable broth variety, use the regular variety with equally delicious results, though the sodium content will be considerably higher.

Some of our recipes do not call for broth enhancers. The soup ingredients will break up a bit as they cook, blending and incorporating in the simmering water to form a flavorful broth without need of enrichment.

We often prepare soups that include beans as well as pasta. The combination of grains and legumes provides a protein-rich meal, and the flavors and textures of these simple foods are quite compatible. We recommend cooking beans in large quantities and freezing whatever isn't used immediately. Next time cooked beans are needed, they will be readily available without resorting to store-bought. (Basic instructions for cooking dried beans appear on page 9.)

We greatly enjoy the texture and flavor of pastina and use it in many of our soups. These various tiny pasta shapes—which can be as small as a grain of rice—are available at well-stocked supermarkets or Italian food stores. They cook very quickly and distribute well among other ingredients to create a soup with a uniform consistency.

If you have leftover cooked noodles, soup is a fine way to use them. Since they are already tender, add them to the pot only a minute or two before serving, just long enough to heat through.

There is a commonly held notion that soup preparation is time-consuming and difficult, requiring prodigious patience and talent. Nothing could be further from the truth. Begin with fresh water or stock and an abundance of vegetables, add noodles and your favorite seasonings, and discover how simple and satisfying the process can be.

Basic Vegetable Noodle Soup

Serve this simple but hearty soup with a crusty whole-grain bread for the perfect winter meal. Don't be alarmed by the amount of garlic indicated in the recipe. It mellows quite magically as it cooks. This soup improves with age for a few days in the refrigerator, or it may be frozen for future use.

Yield: 8 main-course servings

Olive oil	3	tablespoons
Onion	1	large, diced
Green bell pepper	1	large, diced
Green cabbage	1	cup, finely diced
Garlic	6	medium cloves, minced
Whole tomatoes	1	28-ounce can
Water	8	cups
Low-sodium vegetable broth cubes	2	
Dried basil	2	tablespoons
Dried oregano	1	tablespoon
Dried thyme	½	teaspoon
Soy sauce	3	tablespoons
Bay leaves	2	
Salt	½	teaspoon
Pepper		A few grinds
Carrots	2	medium, diced
Mushrooms	½	pound, sliced
Broccoli, chopped	3	cups, loosely packed
Dried pastina	¼	cup
Parmesan cheese, finely grated	1	cup
Dried pasta	8	ounces

Recommended pasta: **egg noodles or any ribbon variety**

Heat the olive oil in a stockpot and sauté the onion, bell pepper, cabbage, and garlic about 5 minutes. Add the tomatoes with their juice and the water, along with the broth cubes, basil, oregano, thyme, soy sauce, bay leaves, salt, and a few grinds of pepper. Bring to a boil over medium heat. Reduce heat and simmer, uncovered, 20 minutes. Add the carrots, mushrooms, and 8 ounces of pasta (not pastina) to the soup and simmer 5 minutes. Add the broccoli and pastina and simmer just until noodles and pastina are tender. Serve with a generous sprinkling of grated Parmesan.

Each serving provides:			
255	Calories	39 g	Carbohydrate
9 g	Protein	763 mg	Sodium
8 g	Fat	27 mg	Cholesterol

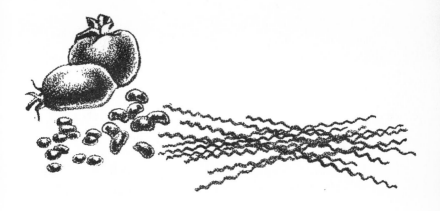

✔ Green Pastina Soup

Simple, nutritious, and delicious, pastina in vegetable and egg broth is at once traditional and thoroughly modern. This makes a light starter course for a dinner party, or a satisfying luncheon main course for 4.

Yield: 6 first-course servings

Fresh chard	1	bunch (about ¾ pound)
Butter	2	tablespoons
Garlic	3	medium cloves, minced
Zucchini	1	medium, finely diced
Water	6	cups
Soy sauce	3	tablespoons
Low-sodium vegetable broth cube	1	
Cayenne pepper	⅛	teaspoon
Dried pastina	½	cup
Egg	1,	lightly beaten
Parmesan cheese, finely grated	½	cup

Carefully wash the chard leaves, spin dry, and chop to yield about 2 cups. Melt the butter in a stockpot and sauté the garlic briefly, then add the chard and zucchini. Stir and sauté 3–4 minutes, until the vegetables begin to release their juices, then add the water, soy sauce, broth cube, and cayenne. Bring to a

simmer over medium-high heat. When bubbling, add the pastina and cook until tender. Turn off the heat and stir the egg into the pot in a slow, thin stream. It will cook as it hits the hot broth and form strands among the pastina and vegetables.*
Serve immediately, passing Parmesan to sprinkle on top.

Each serving provides:

151	Calories	15 g	Carbohydrate
7 g	Protein	621 mg	Sodium
7 g	Fat	53 mg	Cholesterol

---

*Due to the controversy concerning raw eggs and salmonella bacteria, add eggs when the soup is very hot, *not* warm.

Cream of Spinach Soup with Stars

Early spring is the perfect time to make this soup. The flavor and texture are light, delicate, and fresh—just like the season. Use young spinach and freshly grated nutmeg, if possible, to achieve the optimum flavor.

Yield: 6 first-course servings

Fresh spinach	½	pound
Butter	3	tablespoons
Onion	1	medium, finely chopped
Garlic	2	medium cloves, minced
Ground cumin	1	teaspoon
Dry sherry	1	tablespoon
Water	4	cups
Low-sodium vegetable broth cube	1	
Salt	¼	teaspoon
Pepper		A few grinds
Dried star pastina	⅓	cup
Lowfat milk	2	cups
Freshly grated nutmeg		A pinch
Lemon peel, finely grated	½	teaspoon
Lemon wedges	1	per serving

Carefully wash the spinach and discard stems. Melt the butter in a stockpot and add the onion, garlic, cumin, and sherry. Sauté about 2 minutes. Add the water, vegetable broth cube, spinach leaves, salt, and pepper. Bring to a boil, cover, and cook 5 minutes. Puree in a blender or food processor; this may need to be done in several batches. Return the soup to the pot and bring back to a boil. Add the pastina, reduce heat, and simmer, uncovered, 5 more minutes. Stir often while the pastina cooks so it does not sink to the bottom. Add the milk, nutmeg, and lemon peel. Heat through and serve with lemon wedges.

Each serving provides:			
155	Calories	15 g	Carbohydrate
6 g	Protein	284 mg	Sodium
8 g	Fat	19 mg	Cholesterol

✔ Pastina and Pea Soup

The preparation time for this soup is so short you can hardly believe it is homemade, from scratch! Serve as a starter course or with French bread and cheese as a quick and delightful lunch or light supper.

Yield: 6 first-course servings

Olive oil	2	tablespoons
Garlic	3	medium cloves, minced
Onion	1	medium, finely diced
Water	6	cups
Low-sodium vegetable broth cubes	2	
Dried tarragon	1	teaspoon
White wine	½	cup
Dried pastina	1	cup
Single cream	½	cup
Peas, fresh or frozen	1	cup
Parmesan cheese, finely grated	½	cup

In a large stockpot, sauté the garlic and onion in the olive oil several minutes. Add the water and vegetable broth cubes and bring to a boil over medium-high heat. Stir in the tarragon and wine, reduce heat, and simmer 5 minutes. Bring back to a boil and add the pastina. Cook 4–5 minutes, until al dente. Stir in the single cream, peas, and Parmesan. Heat through and serve.

Each serving provides:

264	Calories	28 g	Carbohydrate
10 g	Protein	235 mg	Sodium
11 g	Fat	14 mg	Cholesterol

Creamy Cauliflower Rosemary Soup with Pastina

This soup was concocted at a moment's notice using the simple ingredients that happened to be on hand. It has become a winter favorite.

Yield: 8 first-course servings

Cauliflower	1	small
Green onions	7	
Butter	2	tablespoons
Dried rosemary	1½	teaspoons
Garlic	2	medium cloves, minced
Mushrooms	½	pound, thickly sliced
Salt	½	teaspoon
Flour	1	tablespoon
Water	2½	cups
Lowfat milk	2½	cups
Brandy	¼	cup
Soy sauce	2	tablespoons
Cayenne pepper	¼	teaspoon
Dried pastina	½	cup
Parmesan cheese, finely grated	1	cup

Cut the cauliflower into bite-size florets and finely dice the stem portion. Remove all but about 2 inches of the green portion of onions, and cut the remainder into 1-inch lengths. Melt the butter in a heavy stockpot over low heat. Add the rosemary and garlic. Stir and sauté 1 minute before adding cauliflower, green onions, and mushrooms. Sprinkle the salt over the vegetables and sauté, stirring occasionally, about 7 minutes. Sprinkle the flour over the contents of the pan and stir to distribute. Add the water, milk, brandy, soy sauce, and cayenne. Cover and bring to a simmer over medium heat. When bubbling, add the pastina and simmer, uncovered, 5 minutes or so, until it is tender. Serve at once with Parmesan to sprinkle on top.

Each serving provides:

192	Calories	16 g	Carbohydrate
10 g	Protein	694 mg	Sodium
8 g	Fat	20 mg	Cholesterol

✔ Carrot Curry Soup with Couscous

This soup is delicate but full-flavored. Be sure to dice the vegetables very finely to achieve the consistency needed to blend the flavors and please the eye.

Yield: 6 main-course servings

Butter	2	tablespoons
Onion	1	small, finely diced
Carrots	3	medium, finely diced
Red bell pepper	1	medium, finely diced
Curry powder	4	teaspoons
Water	6	cups
Low-sodium vegetable broth cubes	2	
Dried couscous	½	cup
Plain lowfat yogurt	1	cup
Lowfat milk	1	cup
Fresh cilantro, minced	2	tablespoons

Melt the butter in a large stockpot. Add the vegetables and sauté over very low heat 3–4 minutes. Stir in the curry powder and cook for a moment or two. Add the water and vegetable broth cubes and bring to a boil. Reduce heat, cover, and simmer 10 minutes. Add the couscous, stir, and cover. Continue to cook 6 minutes. Meanwhile, whisk together the yogurt and milk in a bowl. Add a few tablespoons of the hot soup to the yogurt mixture and stir in. Add a little more hot soup, and stir again. The idea is to gradually heat the yogurt so it does not curdle when added to the soup. When a warm, thin consistency is achieved, stir the yogurt mixture into the soup. Heat through. Stir in the cilantro and serve.

Each serving provides:

178	Calories	23 g	Carbohydrate
7 g	Protein	172 mg	Sodium
6 g	Fat	14 mg	Cholesterol

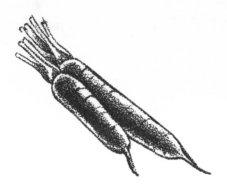

Spicy Zucchini Noodle Soup with Avocado Salsa

You will enjoy the interplay of textures created when this hot soup is topped with the fresh salsa.

Yield: 6 main-course servings

The salsa

Cumin seeds	1	teaspoon
Avocado, firmly ripe	1	medium, peeled and diced
Lemon juice	2	tablespoons
Fresh tomatoes	2	medium, diced
Green onions	3	
Garlic	1	medium clove, minced
Salt	¼	teaspoon
Cayenne pepper	⅛	teaspoon

The soup

Olive oil	2	tablespoons
Garlic	3	medium cloves, minced
Chili powder	½	teaspoon
Ground cumin	1	teaspoon
Onion	1	large, coarsely chopped
Zucchini	2	medium, diced
Red bell pepper	1	small, diced
Dried tomatoes, slivered	¼	cup, loosely packed
Fresh cilantro, minced	¼	cup
Water	3	cups
Salt	½	teaspoon
Buttermilk or plain lowfat yogurt	1	cup
Parmesan cheese, finely grated	½	cup
Dried pasta	12	ounces

Recommended pasta: whole wheat ribbons, spirals, or shells

An hour or two before serving time, make the salsa. You must use perfectly ripe tomatoes and avocado. The tomatoes should be a uniform bright red and the avocado should yield easily but only slightly to pressure when squeezed. Toast the cumin seeds (see page 20) and set aside. Toss the avocado with the lemon juice. Add the tomatoes with their juice, to the avocado. Slice the white portion of the onions and a couple of inches of the green into very thin rounds. Add to the salsa, along with the cumin seeds, garlic, salt, and cayenne. Stir gently to combine well, then cover and set aside at room temperature so the flavors can blend.

Half an hour before serving time, put pasta water on to boil in a pot other than the one you will use for the soup. Heat the olive oil in a stockpot, add the garlic, chili powder, and ground cumin, and stir for a moment or two before adding the onion, zucchini, bell pepper, dried tomatoes, and cilantro. Sauté over medium high heat 5 minutes, stirring frequently. Add the water and the salt, bring to a boil, reduce heat, and simmer, uncovered, 10 minutes. Meanwhile, boil the noodles in the pasta water until al dente. Drain well and keep warm until needed. When the soup cooking time is up, whisk a few tablespoons of the hot broth into a bowl with the buttermilk or yogurt, then add the mixture slowly to the soup. Immediately turn off the heat, add half the Parmesan, and stir. Divide the noodles between 6 large bowls. Ladle the soup over the noodles, scoop a good amount of the salsa on top, and sprinkle with a little Parmesan.

Each serving provides:

392	Calories	57 g	Carbohydrate
16 g	Protein	490 mg	Sodium
14 g	Fat	8 mg	Cholesterol

✔ Pesto Tortellini Soup

This soup has a sensual feel to it; a great meal for a quiet, romantic evening. Serve with a butter leaf salad and a chardonnay.

Yield: 2 main-course servings

Fresh spinach and cheese tortellini	3 ounces
Water	1½ cups
Low-sodium vegetable broth cube	½ cube
Lowfat milk (2%)	½ cup
Basil Pesto	¼ cup (see page 32)
Fresh basil leaves (optional; for garnish)	Several leaves

Bring a quart of water to a boil and cook the tortellini until al dente. Drain and set aside. Combine the water, the vegetable broth cube, milk, and pesto in a medium-size pan and bring to a simmer over medium heat. Add the cooked tortellini and simmer a moment longer. Remove from the heat, garnish with the fresh basil, and serve.

Each serving provides:

342	Calories	31 g	Carbohydrate
16 g	Protein	454 mg	Sodium
19 g	Fat	35 mg	Cholesterol

Soba in Broth with Fried Vegetables and *Age*

This dish calls for the puffy deep-fried tofu called age. *Asian markets carry it fresh, often in bulk. Do not substitute the canned variety. If you are unable to find fresh* age, *use cubed firm tofu in its place. You can substitute vermicelli if you can't locate buckwheat soba.*

Yield: 4 main-course servings

The soba topping

Roasted sesame oil	1	tablespoon
Olive oil	2	tablespoons
Garlic	4	medium cloves, minced
Dried red chili flakes	½	teaspoon
Green onions	3	
Carrot	1	large, thinly sliced
Broccoli, chopped	3	cups, loosely packed
Green cabbage, diced	2	cups
Age, diced	2	cups
Salt	¼	teaspoon
Fresh cilantro, minced	¼	cup
Soba or vermicelli	8	ounces

The broth

Sesame seeds	2	tablespoons
Water	3	cups, plus ¼ cup
Mirin or sweet sherry	¼	cup
Low-sodium vegetable broth cube	1	
Soy sauce	1	tablespoon
Miso	1	tablespoon

Put several quarts of water on to boil for the soba. Use the white portion of the onions and about 2 inches of the green, cut into 1-inch lengths. Heat the oils in a high-walled skillet. Sauté the garlic and chili flakes a few moments, then add the onions and carrot. Stir and sauté over medium heat 5 minutes. Add the broccoli, cabbage, *age,* and salt. Stir and sauté 10 minutes longer (you want the vegetables to brown a bit). Turn off the heat, stir in the cilantro, and set aside. Meanwhile, put the soba in the boiling water and cook until soft; buckwheat flour can have a gritty texture when not completely cooked.

While the noodles cook, make the broth. Toast the sesame seeds (see page 20). In a medium-size saucepan combine 3 cups water with the mirin, broth cube, toasted sesame seeds, and soy sauce. Heat to a simmer. Meanwhile, whisk the miso with ¼ cup water until a smooth paste consistency is achieved. When the broth is simmering, turn off the heat and stir in the miso paste. A beautiful cloudy effect will result. Warm 4 deep bowls. Divide the cooked and drained soba among the bowls. Ladle broth into the bowls to just cover the noodles. Top with fried vegetables and serve. You can pass additional soy sauce at the table, if you wish.

Each serving provides:

888	Calories*	67 g	Carbohydrate
37 g	Protein	719 mg	Sodium
55 g	Fat	0 mg	Cholesterol

---

*Because this is high in calories, you might want to save this for a special occasion.

French Onion Soup with Pasta

This soup could also be served as a hearty main course for 4. For us, it has replaced the traditional chicken noodle soup as the cure for the common cold, but you do not need to be sick to enjoy it.

Yield: 8 first-course servings

Canola oil	¼	cup
Onions	5	medium, coarsely chopped
Bay leaves	2	whole
Water	2	cups, plus 8 cups
Soy sauce	2	tablespoons
Worcestershire sauce	1	tablespoon
Tabasco sauce (optional)	⅛	teaspoon
Low-sodium vegetable broth cubes	3	
Lemon peel, finely grated	½	teaspoon
Jarlsberg cheese, grated (optional)	1½	cups
Dried pasta	1	cup

Recommended pasta: any small soup pasta such as small shells or tripolini

Heat the oil in a large stockpot over medium heat. Add the onions and bay leaves; reduce heat and cook gently, stirring often, about 10 minutes, until the onions are translucent and golden (do not brown them). Meanwhile, in a small saucepan, bring 2 cups water to a boil; add the soy sauce, Worcestershire,

Tabasco, and broth cubes. When the onions are golden, remove the bay leaves and add the lemon peel. Pour in the broth mixture and 8 additional cups water. Bring to a boil, then reduce heat. Simmer, covered, over low heat 1¼ hours. Remove the lid, increase the heat to a boil, add the pasta, and cook until al dente. Ladle the soup into individual ovenproof serving bowls. Top with the cheese and place under the grill for a minute or so to melt it. Serve immediately. (This soup is also delightful without the cheese.)

	Each serving provides:		
180	Calories	21 g	Carbohydrate
5 g	Protein	367 mg	Sodium
8 g	Fat	0 mg	Cholesterol

Savory Pumpkin and Pasta Soup

Pumpkin is high in beta carotene and fiber, which makes it especially nutritious. This recipe calls for canned pumpkin because it is available all year, but you can use cooked and pureed fresh pumpkin. The soup's flavor is wonderful, its texture light and creamy. We suggest either of two different garnishes. The toasted walnuts lend a woodsy accent that complements the nutmeg and allspice. Try the cilantro and lemon for a lighter, summer version. Serve with a merlot and hot rolls.

Yield: 6 main-course servings

Pumpkin	1	29-ounce can or 4 cups fresh puree
Garlic	2	medium cloves, minced
Water	3½	cups
Low-sodium vegetable broth cube	1	
Lowfat milk	2	cups
Dried pastina	¼	cup
Ground nutmeg		Scant ⅛ teaspoon
Ground allspice		Scant ⅛ teaspoon
Salt and pepper		To taste
Fresh parsley, finely minced	¾	cup
Romano cheese, finely grated	1	cup
Butter	3	tablespoons
Plain lowfat yogurt	1	cup

For garnish

Raw walnuts, minced	¼	cup
or		
Fresh cilantro, minced	⅓	cup
Lemon wedges	1	per serving

In a large stockpot, combine the pumpkin, garlic, water, vegetable broth cube, and milk. Bring to a boil and stir in the pastina. Cook until al dente, about 7 minutes, then add the nutmeg, allspice, salt, pepper, and parsley. Remove the pan from the heat and stir in the Romano and butter. Whisk a few tablespoons of hot soup into the yogurt. Whisk in a few more tablespoons of hot soup. The idea is to gradually heat the yogurt so it does not curdle when added to the soup. When a warm, thin consistency is achieved, stir the yogurt mixture into the soup. Serve immediately in heated bowls with the garnish of your choice. If you plan to offer the walnut garnish, toast the chopped walnuts ahead of time (see page 20).

Each serving provides:

257	Calories	27 g	Carbohydrate
12 g	Protein	333 mg	Sodium
12 g	Fat	35 mg	Cholesterol

Caldo Verde with Pasta and Port

A traditional Portuguese soup is transformed from humble to haute with the addition of port wine and pasta. Yes, it is a lot of garlic, but it mellows completely as it cooks and softens. As the name implies, the finished soup is a lovely spring green, so use a white noodle for color contrast. This soup is quite hearty, perfect for a cold evening when you want a meal that sticks to the ribs.

Yield: 8 main-course servings

Fresh kale	½ pound
Garlic	1 bulb (12 medium cloves)
Russet potatoes	2 pounds, peeled and diced
Onion	1 large, coarsely chopped
Water	6 cups
Salt	1 teaspoon
Pepper	A few grinds
Olive oil	3 tablespoons
Port	¾ cup
Parmesan cheese, finely grated	3 tablespoons
Lemon wedges	1 per serving
Dried pasta	8 ounces

Recommended pasta: egg noodles are ideal, or any ribbon broken into short lengths

Wash the kale, discard the toughest part of the stems, and tear leaves into large pieces. Break the garlic bulb into individual cloves and peel them. In a stockpot, combine the potatoes, onion, kale, whole garlic cloves, and water. Stir in the salt and a few grinds of pepper and bring to a boil over medium-high heat. Reduce heat to low and simmer, covered, an hour or so, until all the vegetables are quite soft. Meanwhile, bring a few quarts of water to a boil in a separate pot and cook the pasta until al dente. Be careful not to overcook, as the slightly chewy texture of the noodles is important to the success of this dish. Drain well, toss with 1 tablespoon of the olive oil, and set aside. Puree the soup in a blender or food processor and return to the pot—this will have to be done in two batches. Whisk port, 2 tablespoons olive oil, and Parmesan into the pureed soup. Taste and add more salt and pepper, if desired. Stir in the cooked noodles and heat through. Serve very hot with lemon wedges and additional Parmesan, if desired.

Each serving provides:

306	Calories	48 g	Carbohydrate
8 g	Protein	342 mg	Sodium
7 g	Fat	29 mg	Cholesterol

Red Lentil and Pasta Soup

*Red lentils are not as common as the brown variety, but they are
worth looking for. Many gourmet food stores carry them, as well as
natural food stores. The flavor is lighter and more delicate, and the
cooking time shorter. This recipe calls for finely chopped onions, and
this is very important to the outcome of the soup. Use a food
processor if you have one. This soup could also be served as a light
but nourishing main course.*

Yield: 6 first-course servings

Red lentils	½	cup
Butter	3	tablespoons
Onion	1	large, finely chopped
Dried chervil	1	teaspoon
Dried tarragon	1	teaspoon
Low-sodium vegetable broth cubes	2	
Hot water	7	cups
Port	½	cup
Dried pastina	½	cup

Sort and rinse the lentils and soak them, covered, in 1 cup boiling water 30 minutes. Meanwhile, melt the butter in a large
stockpot over low heat and sauté the onion about 4 minutes,

until golden. Add the chervil and tarragon; stir to distribute. Dissolve the broth cubes in 2 cups hot water and pour it into the soup pot. Add the remaining 5 cups hot water and bring to a boil. Pour in the lentils, along with their soaking liquid, and return to a boil. Reduce heat. Simmer, uncovered, until lentils are soft, about 25 minutes. Bring the pot back to a strong boil and stir in the pastina. Continue to cook about 4 minutes, until the pastina is al dente. Stir in the port and serve in heated bowls.

Each serving provides:

227	Calories	27 g	Carbohydrate
8 g	Protein	135 mg	Sodium
7 g	Fat	16 mg	Cholesterol

Tomato Cannellini Bean Soup with Noodles

The body of this soup is thick and chunky. It is sure to satisfy large appetites. Cannellini beans are available in any Italian grocery store. If you are unable to find them, substitute navy beans.

Yield: 6 main-course servings

Dried cannellini or navy beans	½	cup
Olive oil	2	tablespoons
Garlic	2	medium cloves, minced
Onion	1	medium, coarsely chopped
Stewed tomatoes	1	16-ounce can
Tomato paste	1	6-ounce can
Water	7	cups
Dried oregano	2	tablespoons
Salt and pepper		To taste
Broccoli florets	2	cups, loosely packed
Mushrooms	½	pound, sliced
Parmesan cheese, finely grated	¾	cup
Dried pasta	½	cup

Recommended pasta: any small soup-style pasta, such as tubes or mini-bowties

Sort and rinse the beans and soak several hours or overnight. Drain. In a large stockpot, gently heat the olive oil. Add the garlic and onion and sauté over low heat several minutes. Add the beans, stewed tomatoes and their liquid, tomato paste, the water, and oregano. Bring to a boil, reduce heat, and simmer 25 minutes, until the beans are tender but not fully cooked, stirring occasionally. Salt and pepper can be added to taste. Add the broccoli and mushrooms to the soup, along with the pasta. Increase the heat to a boil, stir, and turn down to a rapid simmer. Simmer until pasta is al dente. Serve very hot, passing the Parmesan.

Each serving provides:

273	Calories	36 g	Carbohydrate
15 g	Protein	660 mg	Sodium
9 g	Fat	10 mg	Cholesterol

Spinach, Lima Bean, and Pasta Soup

The blending of red, white, and green in this soup pleases the eye as much as the flavors please the palate. Make it when you find really fresh and beautiful spinach at the market.

Yield: 8 main-course servings

The beans

Dried lima beans	2	cups
Bay leaves	3	
Garlic	1	large clove, crushed

The soup

Fresh spinach	2	bunches (about 1½ pounds)
Olive oil	3	tablespoons
Red bell pepper	1	medium, coarsely chopped
Onion	1	medium, coarsely chopped
Garlic	2	medium cloves, minced
Dried basil	1	tablespoon
Salt	½	teaspoon
Water	4	cups
Soy sauce	2	tablespoons
Cayenne pepper	¼	teaspoon
Parmesan cheese, finely grated	½	cup
Dried pasta	8	ounces

Recommended pasta: shells, bowties, or spirals

Sort and rinse the beans and soak several hours or overnight. Drain off the soaking water and boil the beans in a quart or so of fresh water 45 minutes, along with the bay leaves and crushed garlic clove. Drain, reserving 2 cups of the cooking liquid. Carefully wash the spinach, discard the stems, and coarsely chop. In a stockpot, heat the olive oil and add the bell pepper, onion, garlic, and basil. Stir and sauté about 5 minutes. Stir in the spinach, sprinkle with the salt, cover, and steam about 5 minutes. Add the beans, 4 cups water, the reserved bean cooking liquid, soy sauce, and cayenne. Simmer, uncovered, over medium heat 15 minutes. Meanwhile, bring a few quarts of water to a boil and cook the pasta until al dente. Drain the pasta and stir it into the soup. Serve hot, passing the Parmesan.

Each serving provides:

248	Calories	34 g	Carbohydrate
11 g	Protein	562 mg	Sodium
8 g	Fat	5 mg	Cholesterol

Minestrone with Rosemary Pesto

Soups are such a wonderful blending of diverse ingredients. This one calls on one unexpected guest, namely Rosemary Pesto!

Yield: 8 main-course servings

Dried cannellini or navy beans	½	cup
Olive oil	3	tablespoons
Celery	3	ribs, finely diced
Onion	1	large, finely diced
Green cabbage, shredded	4	cups
Carrot	1	large, finely diced
Stewed tomatoes	1	16-ounce can
Bay leaves	3	
Salt and pepper		To taste
Water	10	cups
Low-sodium vegetable broth cube	1	
Rosemary Pesto	4	tablespoons (see page 33)
Dried pasta	½	cup

Recommended pasta: any small soup shape, such as shells, bowties, or tripolini

Soak the beans several hours or overnight. Drain. Heat the olive oil in a large stockpot. Sauté the celery and onion a few minutes, until just tender. Add the beans, cabbage, carrot, and stewed tomatoes. Cook over low heat several minutes, stirring often. Add 8 cups water, broth cube, bay leaves, salt, and pepper. Bring to a boil over medium heat. Reduce heat, cover, and simmer 1¼ hours. Stir occasionally. When the beans are tender, add 2 cups boiling water and the pasta. Bring to a rapid simmer and cook until pasta is al dente. Stir in the pesto. Remove from the heat and let stand a few minutes before serving.

Each serving provides:

203	Calories	23 g	Carbohydrate
6 g	Protein	227 mg	Sodium
10 g	Fat	1 mg	Cholesterol

Two-Bean Zuppa

Here, the simple ingredients produce a hearty, stewlike soup that is very filling. If you want to make it in a hurry, substitute canned beans for the dried ones. One cup of each bean will do; drain and rinse before using.

Yield: 6 main-course servings

Dried garbanzo beans (chickpeas)	½	cup
Dried kidney beans	½	cup
Water	10	cups
Low-sodium vegetable broth cube	1	
Olive oil	3	tablespoons
Onions	2	medium, finely diced
Garlic	4	medium cloves, minced
Canned stewed tomatoes	1	cup
Basil Pesto	½	cup (see page 32)
Lowfat milk	1	cup
Dried pasta	1	cup

Recommended pasta: ziti or other small tube variety

Sort and rinse the beans and soak them several hours or overnight. Drain. Combine beans, 8 cups water, and the vegetable broth cube in a large pot. Bring to a boil. Reduce heat and maintain at a simmer. Heat the olive oil in a skillet and sauté the onions and garlic until the onions are just transparent. Add to the beans and cook about 45 minutes, until the beans are soft but not mushy. Stir in the tomatoes and pesto; simmer, uncovered, 10 minutes. Bring up to a boil; add 2 cups boiling water and the pasta. Cook until the pasta is al dente, stirring occasionally. Just before serving, add the milk and heat through.

Each serving provides:

410	Calories	46 g	Carbohydrate
16 g	Protein	325 mg	Sodium
19 g	Fat	6 mg	Cholesterol

Curried Tomato Soup with Pasta and Garbanzos

This beautiful red soup is hearty and warming—perfect for a rainy day.

Yield: 8 main-course servings

The beans

Dried garbanzo beans (chickpeas)	1	cup
Garlic	3	medium cloves, crushed
Bay leaves	2	
Dried red chili flakes	1	teaspoon

The soup

Butter	3	tablespoons
Garlic	4	medium cloves, minced
Onion	1	medium, coarsely chopped
Dried thyme	1	teaspoon
Curry powder	2–3	tablespoons
Carrots	2	medium, diced
Zucchini	1	medium, diced
Green bell pepper	1	medium, finely chopped

Broccoli, chopped	3	cups, loosely packed
Whole tomatoes	1	28-ounce can
Water	9	cups
Soy sauce	2	tablespoons
Salt	½	teaspoon
Cayenne		To taste
Dry red wine	1	cup
Plain lowfat yogurt	1	cup
Dried pasta	8	ounces

Recommended pasta: small shells, elbows, or tubes

Sort and rinse the beans and soak several hours or overnight. Drain. Cover beans with fresh water in a large pot. Add the crushed garlic, bay leaves, and chili flakes. Cover and simmer 1 hour, or until beans are tender but not mushy. Drain the beans and set aside.

Melt the butter in a stockpot, add the garlic, onion, thyme, and 2 tablespoons curry powder (the total amount of curry you use will depend on the intensity of the brand you buy). Stir and sauté a minute or two, then add the carrots, zucchini, bell pepper, and broccoli. Stir and sauté about 5 minutes longer. Add the tomatoes, water, soy sauce, and salt. Add a little cayenne pepper or additional curry powder if you want a spicier soup. Bring the soup to a simmer over medium-high heat. Meanwhile, boil a few quarts of water in a separate pot and cook the pasta until al dente. Drain well, toss with a table-spoon of olive oil, and set aside. When soup is simmering, add the wine and cooked garbanzos and cook, uncovered, 5 minutes. Turn off the heat and stir in the cooked pasta. Whisk a few tablespoons of hot soup broth into the yogurt in a small bowl. Add a few more tablespoons of hot soup and whisk again. The idea is to heat the yogurt gradually so it does not curdle when added to the soup. When a warm, thin consistency is achieved, gently stir it into the soup. Serve very hot.

	Each serving provides:		
335	Calories	51 g	Carbohydrate
13 g	Protein	646 mg	Sodium
7 g	Fat	13 mg	Cholesterol

Pasta Salads

Like its cousin, potato salad, macaroni salad has long been an American picnic standard. Gradually, the classic version—dominated by celery, egg, and mayonnaise—is being replaced by lighter, more inventive concoctions. No longer loyal to old-fashioned elbow and short tube noodles for salad, we draw on a vast array of pasta shapes as inspiration for innovative cold feasts.

Oil is an important component in most pasta salads. We commonly use extra virgin olive oil, which adds a robust olive aroma and flavor. Gourmet oils, such as walnut and sesame, also add distinctive accents that can lend special character to a dish. They are quite powerful, so a little goes a long way.

Specialty vinegars infuse a salad with delicate but unique flavors. They are available in vast variety at well-stocked gourmet food stores, or you can easily make your own. Pack a jar with your choice of herbs and a few peeled and sliced garlic cloves. Cover with heated wine vinegar and cap tightly. Put the jars in a bright spot in your kitchen and let them stand several days, then strain the vinegar through cheesecloth into sterilized decorative jars. Store them in your basement or kitchen cupboard until ready to use. A sprig or two of the fresh herb can be placed in each jar for easy visual identification.

Also deserving mention is rice wine vinegar, available at Asian specialty food stores, which imparts a subtle sweetness. Balsamic vinegar from the Mediterranean region is another distinctive vinegar you may wish to keep on hand for its mellow, woody flavor.

Naturally, a great pasta salad begins with perfectly cooked pasta. Cook it in plenty of boiling water until it is al dente, then cool it by plunging it into a bowl of cold water for a few moments. Drain it well so your flavorful dressing won't be diluted. If you have cooked the noodles before the other salad components are ready, toss them with a little olive oil and set aside— at room temperature if they will be held under an hour, in the refrigerator if longer. Combine the cooled noodles with the other ingredients and toss gently, but thoroughly, to distribute everything evenly. Serve immediately, or allow the salad to marinate a few hours first so the flavors can combine and ripen.

We recommend that pasta salads, particularly those with creamy dressings, be held in the refrigerator if they are not to be eaten immediately. Before serving, allow the refrigerated salad to sit at room temperature an hour or so. The flavors will relax and expand as the salad warms slightly, and the sauce will return to a perfect smooth consistency.

Salads containing raw sliced or chopped mushrooms should marinate no longer than two hours or so, as mushrooms can turn rubbery and darken the mixture to an unappetizing brown. If your salad contains nuts, you may wish to hold them out and add them just before serving to preserve their crunch.

Since macaroni salads are most often served in combination with other foods, at a picnic or a potluck, our suggested serving sizes reflect this. These salads are delicious enough, however, to serve as a main course when you're in the mood for a light and refreshing repast.

So many delicious combinations of flavor, color, and texture are possible. We hope the diversity of salad styles we present here will encourage you to experiment in your own kitchen joyfully and fearlessly.

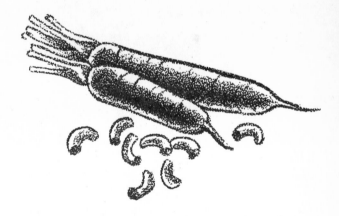

Summer-Fresh Pasta Salad

This salad is lightly dressed with a creamy pesto dressing. The fresh vegetables give it a wonderful light texture and flavor. Make it ahead of time so the flavors can blend, but don't hold it overnight, as the pesto discolors the noodles.

Yield: 6 side-dish servings

The dressing

Mayonnaise	½ cup
Light sour cream	½ cup
Basil Pesto	¼ cup (see page 32)

The salad

Olive oil	1 tablespoon
Celery	2 ribs, diced
Red onion, finely diced	½ cup
Black olives, chopped	⅓ cup
Zucchini	1 medium, diced
Fresh parsley, minced	1 cup
Dried pasta	8 ounces

Recommended pasta: spirals or shells

Whisk together the dressing ingredients and refrigerate to allow flavors to blend while you prepare the rest of the salad. Cook the pasta until al dente. Cool in a bowl of cold water and drain well. Transfer to a large bowl and drizzle with the olive oil. Toss gently to coat the noodles. Add the remaining ingredients and toss well to distribute everything evenly. Pour the dressing over the salad and toss to combine.

Each serving provides:

403	Calories	36 g	Carbohydrate
9 g	Protein	240 mg	Sodium
26 g	Fat	20 mg	Cholesterol

Pasta Salad with Broccoli and Mustard Seeds

This salad combines a considerable quantity of vegetables with the pasta, so it does not come across as too starchy. A great light picnic salad.

Yield: 8 side-dish servings

The dressing

Mustard seeds	1	tablespoon
Olive oil	½	cup
Water	¼	cup
Garlic	1	medium clove, minced
Capers, with juice	3	tablespoons
Lemon juice	3	tablespoons
Salt	¼	teaspoon
Pepper		A few grinds

The salad

Broccoli florets	3	cups, loosely packed
Broccoli stems, peeled and diced	1	cup
Red bell pepper	1	medium, finely diced
Mushrooms	½	pound, thinly sliced
Parmesan cheese, finely grated	¼	cup
Dried pasta	8	ounces

Recommended pasta: spirals or tubes

The vegetables should marinate in the dressing a few hours before being combined with the pasta, so begin to prepare the salad well ahead of time. Toast the mustard seeds (see page 20). Whisk together the dressing ingredients until smooth. Set aside. Put a few inches of water in a lidded pot and place a steaming rack over the water. Bring the water to a boil and steam the broccoli florets 3–4 minutes, until barely tender. Cool in a bowl of cold water. Drain well and combine with the raw diced broccoli stems, bell pepper, and dressing in a large bowl. Toss to coat evenly and marinate in the refrigerator. This can be done up to a day in advance. When ready to serve, bring marinated vegetables to room temperature. Cook the pasta until al dente, cool in a bowl of cold water, drain, and toss with the marinated vegetables, the mushrooms, and the cheese.

Each serving provides:			
270	Calories	27 g	Carbohydrate
7 g	Protein	225 mg	Sodium
16 g	Fat	2 mg	Cholesterol

Pasta Salad with Pesto and Peas

This is a nice fresh-tasting summer salad, perfect to take along on a picnic.

Yield: 8 side-dish servings

The dressing

Mayonnaise	1½	cups
Basil Pesto	¼	cup (see page 32)
Lemon juice	¼	cup
Garlic	2	medium cloves, minced

The salad

Olive oil	1	tablespoon
Romano cheese, finely grated	1	cup
Black olives, chopped	½	cup, firmly packed
Cucumber	1	large, peeled, seeded, diced
Mushrooms	½	pound, sliced
Peas, fresh or frozen	1½	cups
Dried pasta	12	ounces

Recommended pasta: spirals or shells

This salad will improve if it marinates several hours in the refrigerator, so make it well ahead of time. If using frozen peas, set them out to thaw before beginning. Whisk together the dressing ingredients. Set aside. Bring a large pan of water to a boil and cook the pasta until al dente. Cool in a bowl of cold water and drain well. Transfer to a large bowl and toss with the olive oil. Add the Romano, olives, cucumber, mushrooms, and peas to the pasta and toss well to distribute the ingredients evenly. Pour the dressing over the salad and toss gently but well to coat every noodle.

	Each serving provides:		
595	Calories	42 g	Carbohydrate
13 g	Protein	510 mg	Sodium
43 g	Fat	37 mg	Cholesterol

Mushrooms, Jarlsberg, and Pasta with Tarragon Citrus Dressing

This delectable raw mushroom feast looks lovely arranged on a platter and garnished with fresh tarragon sprigs and lemon wedges.

Yield: 8 side-dish servings

The dressing

Olive oil	⅓ cup
Lemon juice	¼ cup
Orange juice	¼ cup
Fresh tarragon leaves, minced	¼ cup
Capers, drained	3 tablespoons
Garlic	2 medium cloves, minced
Prepared mustard	½ teaspoon
Salt	¼ teaspoon
Pepper	A few grinds

The salad

Olive oil	1 tablespoon
Mushrooms	¾ pound, thinly sliced
Jarlsberg cheese	8 ounces, coarsely grated
Dried pasta	8 ounces

Recommended pasta: penne, spirals, or medium shells

Make the dressing first so the flavors can blend. Puree the dressing ingredients in a food processor or blender. Set aside at room temperature. Bring a pot of water to a boil and cook the pasta until al dente. Cool in a bowl of cold water and drain well. Toss with the olive oil in a large bowl. Toss gently with the mushrooms and cheese, then add dressing and toss again.

Each serving provides:

315	Calories	26 g	Carbohydrate
12 g	Protein	295 mg	Sodium
18 g	Fat	18 mg	Cholesterol

Tortellini Salad with Roasted Walnuts

We usually serve macaroni salads as a side dish; however, this stuffed pasta salad makes a satisfying meal in itself. Make it several hours before serving so it can sit at room temperature to allow the flavors to combine. If you wish to make it the night before, refrigerate then let it return to room temperature before serving. The recipe sounds like it has a lot of steps, but it is really very easy to prepare.

Yield: 4 main-course servings

The dressing

Walnut oil	⅓	cup
Wine vinegar	3	tablespoons
Salt and pepper		To taste

The nuts

Olive oil	2	tablespoons
Garlic	2	medium cloves, minced
Raw walnuts, chopped	½	cup
Salt and pepper		To taste

The salad

Fresh parsley, minced	½	cup
Green bell pepper, finely diced	¼	cup
Red bell pepper, finely diced	⅓	cup
Red onion, finely diced	¼	cup
Celery	1	rib, finely diced
Parmesan cheese, finely grated	½	cup
Fresh cheese tortellini	9	ounces

Whisk together the dressing ingredients. Set aside. Heat the olive oil in a small heavy skillet. Add the garlic and cook briefly. Add the walnuts and cook several minutes, stirring frequently. Lightly season with salt and pepper. When walnuts turn golden brown, remove from the heat and drain on paper towels to remove most of the oil. Set aside. Bring several quarts of water with a bit of oil in it to a boil. Cook the tortellini until al dente, drain, and shake gently to remove as much water as possible. In a large bowl, combine the tortellini, parsley, and diced vegetables. Pour the dressing over the salad and toss. Add the walnuts and Parmesan and toss again, gently. (If making this salad well ahead of time, hold out the walnuts and add them just before serving.)

Each serving provides:

577	Calories	36 g	Carbohydrate
18 g	Protein	526 mg	Sodium
41 g	Fat	45 mg	Cholesterol

Cold Pasta in Creamy Garlic Cucumber Sauce

This salad is for garlic lovers only! Serve small portions as a pungent side dish or as the first course of a strongly seasoned feast.

Yield: 8 side-dish servings

Cumin seeds	1	tablespoon
Plain lowfat yogurt	1½	cups
Garlic	4	medium cloves, minced
Red wine vinegar	1	tablespoon
Salt	½	teaspoon
Pepper		A few grinds
Cucumbers	2	large, peeled and seeded
Dried tomatoes, slivered	¼	cup, loosely packed
Parmesan cheese, finely grated	½	cup
Dried pasta	12	ounces

Recommended pasta: wagon wheels, spirals, or tubes

Make the salad and refrigerate a few hours ahead of serving time, if possible, so the flavors will blend and ripen. Put several quarts of water on to boil for the pasta. Toast the cumin seeds (see page 20). Whisk together the cumin seeds, yogurt, garlic, vinegar, salt, and pepper. Grate the cucumbers into the yogurt mixture and stir in the dried tomatoes and Parmesan. Cook the pasta until al dente, cool in a bowl of cold water, and drain well. In a serving bowl, toss the cooled noodles with the yogurt-cucumber sauce.

Each serving provides:			
231	Calories	39 g	Carbohydrate
11 g	Protein	290 mg	Sodium
3 g	Fat	7 mg	Cholesterol

Spicy Aubergine Pasta Salad with Calamata Olives

We find the balance of sweet, sour, and spicy just right in this distinctive salad. We set out to duplicate a dish we had enjoyed at a gourmet lunch counter in Berkeley. Our own ideas took over and it turned out not the same at all, though just as delicious. This dish is interesting and rich enough to carry a meal as a main course.

Yield: 8 main-course servings

Aubergines	2	small (about 1½ pounds)
Green onions	7	
Olive oil	7	tablespoons
Garlic	4	medium cloves, minced
Dried red chili flakes	1	teaspoon
Red bell pepper	1	medium, thinly sliced
Dried oregano	1	teaspoon
Salt	¾	teaspoon
Lemon juice	¼	cup
Balsamic vinegar	1	tablespoon
Mirin or sweet sherry	2	tablespoons
Calamata olives, slivered	½	cup
Fresh parsley, minced	½	cup
Dried pasta	1	pound

Recommended pasta: rigatoni, penne, or other large tubes

Peel the aubergine and cut it into ¼-inch-thick strips about 3 inches in length. Trim all but about 2 inches of the tops from the green onions. Cut in half lengthwise, then into 1-inch pieces. Bring several quarts of water to a boil. Cook the pasta until al dente. Cool in a bowl of cold water, drain well, and toss with 1 tablespoon of the olive oil. Set aside.

Heat 2 tablespoons of the olive oil in a heavy skillet. Add the garlic and chili flakes and stir to distribute in the oil. Add the aubergine, green onion, and bell pepper; stir. Sprinkle with the oregano and ¼ teaspoon of the salt. Stir and sauté over medium-high heat 15–20 minutes, until vegetables are tender and browning nicely. Transfer to a bowl. Meanwhile, whisk together the remaining 4 tablespoons olive oil, the lemon juice, vinegar, mirin, and remaining ½ teaspoon salt. Pour this dressing over the aubergine mixture in the bowl and let the flavors combine for several hours before tossing with the cooled pasta, the olives, and parsley.

Each serving provides:			
386	Calories	52 g	Carbohydrate
9 g	Protein	513 mg	Sodium
16 g	Fat	0 mg	Cholesterol

✔ Pastina Salad with Romaine and Feta

Serve this full-flavored salad as a first course, or make a meal of it with French bread and cheese.

Yield: 4 side-dish servings

The dressing
Olive oil	2	tablespoons
Red wine vinegar	1	tablespoon
Sugar	1	teaspoon
Single cream	1	tablespoon

The salad
Romaine lettuce, torn	2	cups
Fresh tomato	1	medium, chopped
Fresh parsley, minced	½	cup
Feta cheese, crumbled	½	cup
Dried pastina	½	cup

Whisk together the olive oil and vinegar until light in color. Add the sugar and single cream; whisk to combine. Set aside. Heat a small pan of water and cook the pastina until al dente.

Pay close attention as this will take only a couple of minutes. Cool in a bowl of cold water and drain well. Set aside. Toss the lettuce, tomato, and parsley gently in a bowl. Add the feta and cooked pastina and toss again to combine. Pour the dressing over the salad, toss, and serve.

Each serving provides:

201	Calories	19 g	Carbohydrate
6 g	Protein	199 mg	Sodium
11 g	Fat	16 mg	Cholesterol

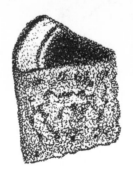

Salad of Olives, Artichokes, Pesto, and Pasta

This dish really hits the spot when you are in the mood for a creamy, rich, cold salad. Make it several hours before mealtime to allow the flavors to combine. Refrigerate it but return it to room temperature before serving. This salad is best eaten the same day it is made so the pesto does not discolor the noodles.

Yield: 6 side-dish servings

The dressing

Basil Pesto	½ cup (see page 32)
Light sour cream	½ cup
Mayonnaise	¼ cup
Lemon juice	1 tablespoon

The salad

Olive oil	1 tablespoon
Marinated artichoke hearts	1 6-ounce jar
Greek black olives, chopped	¼ cup
Green onions	3, minced
Fresh parsley, minced	½ cup
Peas, fresh or frozen	1 cup
Dried pasta	8 ounces

Recommended pasta: spirals or shells

If using frozen peas, set out to thaw ahead of time. Whisk together the dressing ingredients and set aside. Bring a large pot of water to a boil and cook the pasta until al dente. Cool in a bowl of cold water and drain well. In a large bowl, toss the pasta gently with the olive oil. Drain the artichokes, reserving their liquid for another use. Dice them and add to the pasta, along with the remaining ingredients. Toss to combine. Spoon on the dressing and toss gently but well to distribute everything evenly.

Each serving provides:			
445	Calories	42 g	Carbohydrate
13 g	Protein	518 mg	Sodium
27 g	Fat	17 mg	Cholesterol

Lentil, Feta, and Olive Pasta Salad

We use French sheep's milk feta, which is rather dry and milder than some versions. It works beautifully with the other traditional Mediterranean foods combined in this feast of a salad. For a perfect meal, serve it with bread sticks or crunchy rolls and, of course, red wine.

Yield: 8 main-course servings

The lentils

Dried lentils	1½	cups
Bay leaves	2	

The dressing

Olive oil	⅔	cup
Red wine vinegar	¼	cup plus 2 tablespoons
Water	¼	cup
Lemon juice	¼	cup
Garlic	2	medium cloves, minced
Dried oregano	1	tablespoon
Salt	½	teaspoon

The salad

Dried tomatoes, slivered	⅓	cup
Calamata olives, coarsely chopped	½	cup
Green bell pepper	1	medium, minced
Feta cheese	8	ounces, crumbled
Parmesan cheese, finely grated	½	cup
Dried pasta	12	ounces

Recommended pasta: tubes or bowties

Sort and rinse the lentils, and cover with 4 cups boiling water in a large bowl. Let sit 2–3 hours at room temperature. Drain and cook in a few cups of fresh water with the bay leaves over medium heat 10–15 minutes, until the lentils are tender but not at all mushy. Rinse with cold water to cool and refrigerate until you are ready to assemble the salad. Whisk the dressing ingredients together and set aside so the flavors can blend. Bring a pot of water to a boil and cook the pasta until al dente. Cool in a bowl of cold water and drain well. Combine the lentils, pasta, dried tomatoes, olives, bell pepper, feta, and Parmesan in a serving bowl. Toss with the dressing. Grind in a little pepper and toss again. You can allow the flavors to blend in the refrigerator for up to a few hours, but bring it to room temperature before serving. Garnish with parsley sprigs, whole olives, and dried tomato strips, if you wish.

Each serving provides:			
572	Calories	59 g	Carbohydrate
23 g	Protein	654 mg	Sodium
28 g	Fat	30 mg	Cholesterol

Greek-Style Pasta Salad
with Tarragon

This salad uses the ingredients traditionally found in a Greek salad, but combines them with pasta instead of lettuce. Use black olives that are on the small side so they distribute well.

Yield: 8 side-dish servings

The dressing

Olive oil	¼	cup
Garlic wine vinegar	2	tablespoons
Lemon juice	3	tablespoons
Dried tarragon	1	tablespoon

The salad

Olive oil	1	tablespoon
Whole pitted black olives	¾	cup
Green olives with pimiento, sliced	½	cup
Green onions	4	minced
Capers, drained	2	tablespoons
Feta cheese	8	ounces, crumbled
Pepper		A few grinds
Dried pasta	1	pound

Recommended pasta: spirals or shells

Whisk together the dressing ingredients and set aside. Bring a large pot of water to a boil and cook the pasta until al dente. Cool in a bowl of cold water and drain well. In a large bowl, toss the pasta gently with 1 tablespoon olive oil, then toss with remaining ingredients until well combined. Pour the dressing over the salad and toss gently but well. Marinate at room temperature an hour or so before serving.

Each serving provides:			
359	Calories	45 g	Carbohydrate
10 g	Protein	564 mg	Sodium
15 g	Fat	15 mg	Cholesterol

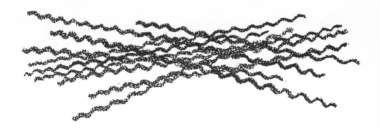

Cold Pasta with Tomatoes, Artichokes, and Capers

This is one of our most popular creations. You must serve it someday to your favorite guests. Complete the meal with crusty garlic bread and red wine.

Yield: 8 main-course servings

Fresh tomatoes	1½	pounds
Marinated artichoke hearts	2	6-ounce jars
Calamata olives, chopped	⅓	cup .
Capers, drained, minced if large	¼	cup
Olive oil	⅓	cup
Garlic	3	medium cloves, minced
Lemon juice	¼	cup
Red wine vinegar	2	tablespoons
Fresh oregano leaves	2	tablespoons
Salt	¼	teaspoon
Cayenne pepper	⅛	teaspoon
Feta cheese	4	ounces, crumbled
Dried pasta	1	pound

Recommended pasta: rigatoni, penne, or other tubes

Put several quarts of water on to boil. Blanch, peel, and seed the tomatoes (see page 21). Chop coarsely and place in a large bowl. Drain the artichokes, reserving their liquid for another use. Cut them into bite-size slivers and add to the tomatoes, along with the remaining ingredients except the feta and pasta. Mix well. This can be done several hours ahead of time and can marinate, covered, at room temperature until you are ready to assemble the salad. Just before mealtime, cook the pasta until al dente in the reheated tomato-blanching water. Cool in a bowl of cold water and drain very well. Combine with the sauce and feta and toss to distribute everything evenly. Serve immediately.

Each serving provides:

393	Calories	51 g	Carbohydrate
11 g	Protein	615 mg	Sodium
17 g	Fat	13 mg	Cholesterol

Cold Vermicelli with Roasted Tomatoes, Fresh Basil, and Eggs

This unusual salad has a light and refreshing effect on the palate when combined on a menu with other hot or cold dishes—at a potluck, for example. Or serve it as the main course of a light meal with crusty garlic bread and red wine.

Yield: 8 side-dish servings

Fresh tomatoes	1½	pounds
Fresh basil leaves	2	cups, loosely packed
Garlic	3	medium cloves, minced
Olive oil	⅔	cup
Red wine vinegar	2	tablespoons
Balsamic vinegar	2	tablespoons
Salt	½	teaspoon
Pepper		To taste
Eggs	2	large, hardboiled
Parmesan cheese, finely grated	½	cup
Dried pasta	1	pound

Recommended pasta: vermicelli or any thin strand

Roast the tomatoes under a hot grill. Use tongs to turn the tomatoes frequently, until they are softening and their skins have blistered, split, and charred. Set aside until they are cool enough to handle, then rub off the skins, cut in half crosswise, and squeeze out the seed pockets. Coarsely chop the tomatoes and place in a large bowl. Coarsely chop the basil and add to the tomatoes. Add the garlic, olive oil, vinegars, salt, and a few grinds of pepper. Stir well. This can be done several hours ahead of time and can marinate, covered, at room temperature until you are ready to assemble the salad. Just before mealtime, put several quarts of water on to boil and cook the pasta until al dente. Cool in a bowl of cold water and drain well. Cut the eggs in half lengthwise and slice each half thinly. Stir into the tomato mixture. Add the pasta to the tomato mixture, stirring and turning gently to distribute the ingredients evenly. Add the Parmesan, toss again, and serve immediately.

Each serving provides:

446	Calories	50 g	Carbohydrate
13 g	Protein	278 mg	Sodium
22 g	Fat	58 mg	Cholesterol

Soba Salad with Carrots, Mangetout Peas, and Sesame Mayo

This pretty salad is a special treat. Do try it with earthy brown soba for an authentic Japanese flavor combination. Or use a thin green strand or ribbon. The contrast in color is an important part of the pleasure of this dish.

Yield: 6 side-dish servings

The dressing

Mayonnaise	⅓	cup
Plain lowfat yogurt	⅓	cup
Firm-style tofu	2	ounces
Mirin or sweet sherry	2	tablespoons
Soy sauce	1	tablespoon
Lemon juice	1	tablespoon
Fresh ginger, grated	1	tablespoon
Sugar	1	teaspoon
Fresh cilantro, minced	¼	cup
Green onions	2	minced

The salad

Mangetout peas	½	pound
Carrot	1	large
Roasted sesame oil	1	tablespoon
Soy sauce	1	tablespoon
Water chestnuts, sliced	½	cup
Sesame seeds	1	tablespoon
Lemon wedges	1	per serving
Dried pasta	8	ounces

Recommended pasta: buckwheat soba, spinach linguine, or fettuccine

In a blender or food processor, puree the mayonnaise, yogurt, tofu, mirin, 1 tablespoon soy sauce, lemon juice, ginger, and sugar to a thin, smooth sauce consistency. Stir the cilantro and green onions into the dressing and set aside. This can be done several hours in advance; the flavors will blend and ripen a little over time. Store the dressing covered in the refrigerator and bring back to room temperature before tossing with the salad ingredients.

When you are ready to assemble the salad, put several quarts of water on to boil for the pasta. Pull the strings from the mangetout peas. Slice the carrot at a slant into very thin oblong discs. When the water is boiling, drop in the pasta and stir. For the last 2 minutes of cooking time, add the mangetout peas and carrots to the pot. (Remember that soba is most delicious cooked a bit beyond the al dente stage, though not until mushy.) Cool the pasta and vegetables in a bowl of cold water, drain well, and toss in a serving bowl with the sesame oil and soy sauce. Toss again with the water chestnuts and the dressing. Toast the sesame seeds (see page 20). Sprinkle the salad with the sesame seeds and garnish with lemon wedges and cilantro sprigs, if desired.

Each serving provides:

329	Calories	42 g	Carbohydrate
9 g	Protein	434 mg	Sodium
14 g	Fat	8 mg	Cholesterol

Pasta Salad Mexicana

Corn elbow macaroni, available in health food markets, has a wonderful texture and flavor that enhance the Mexican theme of this salad. If you can't find the corn variety, make it anyway, using another recommended pasta.

Yield: 8 side-dish servings

The dressing

Avocados, very ripe	2 large
Fresh cilantro, minced	⅓ to ½ cup
Mayonnaise	¼ cup
Plain lowfat yogurt	¼ cup
Lemon juice	3 tablespoons
Balsamic vinegar	2 tablespoons
Soy sauce	1 tablespoon
Dried oregano	2 teaspoons
Chili powder	½ teaspoon
Garlic powder	½ teaspoon

The salad

Fresh tomatoes	2 large, coarsely chopped
Green bell pepper	1 large, finely diced
Red cabbage, diced	½ cup
Broccoli, chopped	3 cups, loosely packed

Carrot	1 large, diced
Red onion	½ large, minced
Black olives, coarsely chopped	1 cup
Raw sunflower seeds	¼ cup
Farmhouse Cheddar cheese	8 ounces, grated
Dried pasta	12 ounces

Recommended pasta: corn elbow macaroni, spirals, or small tubes

Mix the dressing first so that the flavors have time to blend. You can whir all the dressing ingredients in a blender or food processor, or mash and whisk in a bowl to a smooth consistency. Set aside in the refrigerator. Cook the noodles until al dente. Cool in a bowl of cold water and drain well. In a large bowl, combine the fresh vegetables and the olives. Add the cooled noodles and toss. Add the dressing and combine well. Toast the sunflower seeds (see page 20). Just before serving, toss the salad again with the sunflower seeds and the cheese.

Each serving provides:

494	Calories	49 g	Carbohydrate
15 g	Protein	536 mg	Sodium
29 g	Fat	35 mg	Cholesterol

Curried Pasta Salad with Currants and Almonds

The unusual blending of sweet and savory in this salad plays delightful tricks on the palate. It is perfect served in small portions as part of a curry feast.

Yield: 8 side-dish servings

The dressing
Plain lowfat yogurt	⅔	cup
Half-and-half	2	tablespoons
Mirin or sweet sherry	2	tablespoons
Salt	¼	teaspoon
Curry powder	2	teaspoons
Cayenne pepper (optional)	⅛	teaspoon
Fresh cilantro, minced	¼	cup
Green onions	3	minced

The salad
Raw slivered almonds	½	cup
Olive oil	1	tablespoon
Currants	½	cup
Dried pasta	8	ounces

Recommended pasta: small shells, elbows, or tubes

Make the dressing well ahead of time so the flavors can blend. Whisk together the yogurt, half-and-half, mirin, salt, and curry powder. Add cayenne or more curry powder if you feel the dressing needs a more spicy bite. Stir in the cilantro and green onions and set aside. When you are ready to assemble the salad, put several quarts of water on to boil for the pasta. Toast the almonds (see page 20). Cook the pasta until al dente. Cool in a bowl of cold water, drain well, and toss with the olive oil in a serving bowl. Toss the toasted almonds and the currants with the pasta, add the dressing, and toss gently to combine well. Garnish with cilantro sprigs, if you wish.

Each serving provides:

256	Calories	35 g	Carbohydrate
9 g	Protein	87 mg	Sodium
10 g	Fat	3 mg	Cholesterol

Couscous Salad with Dried-Tomato Vinaigrette

Though this salad has many steps, it is not difficult to prepare. The balance of sweet, smoky, and spicy is delicious.

Yield: 6 side-dish servings

The dressing

Olive oil	⅓	cup
Red wine vinegar	3	tablespoons
Dried oregano	1	teaspoon
Salt	¼	teaspoon
Cayenne pepper	⅛	teaspoon
Mustard seeds	1	tablespoon
Cumin seeds	1	tablespoon
Dried tomato, minced	⅓	cup
Fresh cilantro, minced	⅓	cup

The salad

Red bell pepper	1	medium
Water	3	cups
Salt	¼	teaspoon
Garlic powder	¼	teaspoon
Butter	1	tablespoon
Dried couscous	2	cups
Cucumber	1	medium, peeled, seeded
Red onion, minced or grated	¼	cup

Well ahead of time, make the dressing so the flavors can blend. Whisk together the olive oil, vinegar, oregano, salt, and cayenne. Toast the mustard and cumin seeds together (see page 20). Stir the hot seeds into the oil mixture (they will sizzle). Add the dried tomato and cilantro. Stir, cover, and set aside at room temperature for up to several hours, until you are ready to assemble the salad. Roast the bell pepper (see page 21). Meanwhile, heat the water in a lidded saucepan until boiling. Stir in the salt, garlic powder, and butter. When butter has melted, stir in the dried couscous. Immediately cover, remove from heat, and let stand 5 minutes. Transfer couscous to a serving bowl, fluff with a fork, and set aside. Finely chop the roasted bell pepper and place in a bowl. Grate the cucumber into the bowl, add the onion and stir. Toss together the vegetables and couscous. Stir the dressing vigorously and add to the salad. Toss to distribute everything evenly.

<table>
<tr><td colspan="4">Each serving provides:</td></tr>
<tr><td>392</td><td>Calories</td><td>55 g</td><td>Carbohydrate</td></tr>
<tr><td>10 g</td><td>Protein</td><td>217 mg</td><td>Sodium</td></tr>
<tr><td>15 g</td><td>Fat</td><td>5 mg</td><td>Cholesterol</td></tr>
</table>

	Each serving provides:		
392	Calories	55 g	Carbohydrate
10 g	Protein	217 mg	Sodium
15 g	Fat	5 mg	Cholesterol

Creamy Couscous Salad

Serve this unusual salad as a starter course mounded on red lettuce leaves, or take it to your next picnic or family gathering. The light texture of the couscous will please everyone. You can substitute white wine vinegar if the tarragon-garlic is not available.

Yield: 6 side-dish servings

The dressing

Mayonnaise	½	cup
Plain lowfat yogurt	⅓	cup
Tarragon-garlic vinegar	3	tablespoons
Capers, drained and minced	1	heaping teaspoon
Garlic powder	½	teaspoon
Salt and pepper		To taste

The salad

Olive oil	1	tablespoon
Butter	1	tablespoon
Garlic	2	medium cloves, minced
Hot water	1½	cups
Low-sodium vegetable broth cube	½	
Dried couscous	1	cup
Red bell pepper	1	medium, minced
Green bell pepper	1	small, minced
Celery	1	rib, minced
Green onions	2	minced
Fresh parsley, minced	¾	cup

Blend together the dressing ingredients and refrigerate. Heat the olive oil and butter in a 2-quart saucepan. Sauté the garlic briefly, then add the water and vegetable broth cube and bring to a boil. Pour in the dried couscous. Immediately cover, remove from heat, and let stand 5 minutes. Transfer to a serving bowl, fluff with a fork, and set aside. Toss the bell peppers, celery, green onions, and parsley with the couscous until well combined. Pour on the dressing and toss again.

Each serving provides:			
310	Calories	29 g	Carbohydrate
6 g	Protein	179 mg	Sodium
19 g	Fat	17 mg	Cholesterol

Vegetable-Based Stovetop Sauces

There are many who think vegetarian cookery must be very limited and therefore boring. On the contrary! The range of textures, colors, and unique flavors found in the plant kingdom is vast and inspiring. Vegetables in all their variety are at the heart of our favorite pasta dishes. Combined with pasta, vegetables are transformed from humble side dish to main attraction.

The golden rule in vegetable cooking is to start with the very fresh. To ensure the finest quality—reassuringly free from pesticides, coloring agents, waxes, and the like—cooks can grow their own. If you have no interest in gardening, learn to recognize freshness at the market.

As with people, a radiant complexion is a sign of health in plants; brightness of color indicates freshness. Texture as well as color should be robust, so select produce that is firm, not limp and rubbery. A high water content is responsible for vegetables' refreshing crispness—dry-looking or withered produce has been too long off the plant.

The nutritious and delicious character of vegetables diminishes rapidly after harvest. Pay attention when selecting market produce—linger over the task—and the cooking will be a great pleasure, the results delectable.

While we most often prefer fresh vegetables, frozen varieties are sometimes appropriate. Specifically, frozen peas, spinach, and corn appear in a few of our recipes.

In this section, we provide some ideas for combining pasta with vegetables. May your own creativity soar.

✔ Burnt Garlic Pasta

Don't let the name throw you. In this case, the garlic and butter are intentionally "burnt" to impart a special flavor.

Yield: 4 side-dish servings

Butter	3	tablespoons
Garlic	4	medium cloves, minced
Olive oil	2	tablespoons
Parmesan cheese, finely grated	½	cup
Dried pasta	8	ounces

Recommended pasta: **medium shells or spirals**

Put several quarts of water on to boil for the pasta. Melt the butter over high heat in a small skillet. Stir in the garlic. Turn off the heat, but continue to stir until the garlic is crisp and brown. Stir in the olive oil, then strain the mixture and discard the garlic. Cook the pasta until al dente, drain well, and transfer to a warm serving bowl. Pour the butter mixture over the pasta and toss with the Parmesan. Serve very hot.

Each serving provides:

407	Calories	44 g	Carbohydrate
13 g	Protein	319 mg	Sodium
20 g	Fat	33 mg	Cholesterol

✔ Poppy Seed Noodles

This recipe will become one of your old favorites in no time. It is so easy to prepare, and tastes so good! Poppy seeds do lose their flavor with age, so be sure to have some fresh ones on hand. They cling nicely to curvy pasta shapes, and add a delightful crunch. This can be served as a side dish, and it also makes a wonderful light meal when accompanied by salad, bread, and cheese.

Yield: 4 side-dish servings

Olive oil	3	tablespoons
Garlic	2	medium cloves, minced
Salt	¼	teaspoon
Poppy seeds	1	tablespoon
Dried pasta	8	ounces

Recommended pasta: spirals or another curvy shape

Bring several quarts of water to a boil, and cook the pasta until al dente. Drain well and transfer to a warm serving bowl. Meanwhile, measure the olive oil into a tiny pan and add the garlic and salt. You do not really sauté the garlic, but simply heat it over medium heat in the oil. This takes only a moment. Pour this over the pasta and toss well to coat. Sprinkle with the poppy seeds and toss again to distribute evenly. Serve immediately.

Each serving provides:

314	Calories	43 g	Carbohydrate
8 g	Protein	140 mg	Sodium
12 g	Fat	0 mg	Cholesterol

Pasta with Parsley and Sweet Roasted Garlic

This dish is much lighter than its well-known cousin, fettuccine Alfredo. The roasted garlic adds a rich but mellow flavor. You will enjoy the results.

Yield: 4 side-dish servings

Garlic	1	large bulb
Olive oil	1	tablespoon plus ½ teaspoon
Light sour cream	⅓	cup
Single cream	¼	cup
Fresh parsley, minced	½	cup
Dry sherry	2	tablespoons
Dried pasta	8	ounces

Recommended pasta: fettuccine or lasagnette

Preheat oven or top oven to 350 degrees F. Cut ¼ inch off the garlic bulb to barely expose the tops of the cloves. Do not peel. Drizzle on about ½ teaspoon olive oil and bake about 30–45 minutes. Bring several quarts of water to a boil for the pasta. When the garlic bulb is very soft, remove it from the oven and cool. Remove the garlic from the skin by squeezing the cloves from the bottom. The garlic will slide out of the cut end as a soft paste. Whisk the garlic paste with the sour cream, single cream, parsley, and sherry in a small saucepan. Stir and cook over very low heat until just heated through. Meanwhile, cook the pasta until al dente, drain well, and toss with 1 tablespoon olive oil in a warm serving bowl. Quickly reheat the garlic sauce, if necessary, toss with the noodles, and serve.

Each serving provides:			
342	Calories	55 g	Carbohydrate
11 g	Protein	44 mg	Sodium
8 g	Fat	6 mg	Cholesterol

✔ Dried-Tomato Carbonara

Dried tomatoes have a meaty texture and smoky flavor that might even fool your favorite carnivore. For this dish, use dried tomatoes that have been reconstituted in olive oil. You can also use the oil from the tomatoes where olive oil is called for in this recipe.

Yield: 6 side-dish servings

Oil-packed dried tomatoes, drained, slivered	½ cup
Eggs	2 large, beaten
Olive oil	⅓ cup
Garlic	2 medium cloves, minced
Red wine vinegar	1 tablespoon
Madeira	2 tablespoons
Parmesan cheese, finely grated	½ cup
Black olives, finely chopped	½ cup
Dried pasta	12 ounces

Recommended pasta: **fettuccine or tagliarini**

Drain as much oil as possible from the tomatoes before slivering. Bring several quarts of water to a boil and cook the pasta until al dente. Drain very well. Meanwhile, in a large bowl, stir together the eggs, olive oil, garlic, red wine vinegar, Madeira, and Parmesan. Pour this mixture over very hot noodles in a warm serving bowl.* Lift and toss to distribute everything evenly. Add the olives and toss again. Serve immediately, passing the pepper grinder and additional Parmesan, if desired.

Each serving provides:

451	Calories	49 g	Carbohydrate
14 g	Protein	284 mg	Sodium
22 g	Fat	77 mg	Cholesterol

---

*Due to the controversy concerning raw eggs and salmonella bacteria, add eggs when the sauce is very hot, *not* warm. For further information, contact your local office of the U.S. Department of Agriculture.

✔ Pasta with Kasseri and Pine Nuts

It is wonderful to live with a man who likes to cook. Guy Hadler created this simple dish one night when there was "nothing to eat." Another of his creative successes was born.

Yield: 6 side-dish servings

Pine nuts	½ **cup**
Olive oil	2 **tablespoons**
Kasseri or Parmesan cheese, finely grated	⅓ **cup**
Dried pasta	12 **ounces**

Recommended pasta: **bowties or spirals**

Bring several quarts of water to a boil and cook the pasta until al dente. Meanwhile, toast the pine nuts (see page 20). Drain the pasta well and toss with the pine nuts, olive oil, and cheese in a warm bowl. Serve immediately.

Each serving provides:

336	Calories	44 g	Carbohydrate
12 g	Protein	104 mg	Sodium
13 g	Fat	4 mg	Cholesterol

✔ Pasta with Cilantro Pesto and Avocado

The cilantro gives this dish a delightful Mexican flavor. Serve it on a summer evening with salsa, chips, and margaritas.

Yield: 4 main-course servings

Raw pumpkin seeds	¼	cup
Cilantro Pesto	1¼	cups (see page 34)
Light sour cream	½	cup
Red bell pepper	1	medium, minced
Avocado, firmly ripe	1	sliced
Dried pasta	12	ounces

Recommended pasta: **medium shells, spirals, or tubes**

Bring several quarts of water to a boil and cook the pasta until al dente. Drain well and transfer to a warm serving bowl. Meanwhile, toast the pumpkin seeds (see page 20) and mince. Stir together the Cilantro Pesto and sour cream. Heat briefly over very low heat. Toss the hot noodles with bell pepper. Add the pesto mixture and toss again. Serve with the avocado slices and minced pumpkin seeds on top.

Each serving provides:

600	Calories	82 g	Carbohydrate
16 g	Protein	70 mg	Sodium
24 g	Fat	0 mg	Cholesterol

Pasta with Many Peppers and Almonds

Make this dish in late summer, when peppers are at their best. The colors satisfy the senses nearly as much as the flavors do.

Yield: 4 main-course servings

Yellow bell pepper	1	large
Red bell pepper	1	large
Fresh red chilies	2	large
Butter	3	tablespoons
Dried red chili flakes	½	teaspoon
Garlic	3	medium cloves, minced
Red onion	1	medium, coarsely chopped
Whole blanched unsalted almonds	½	cup
Salt	¼	teaspoon
Pepper		A few grinds
Dried oregano	1	teaspoon
Fresh parsley, minced	¼	cup, firmly packed
Dry sherry	⅓	cup
Parmesan cheese, finely grated	⅓	cup
Dried pasta	12	ounces

Recommended pasta: linguine, fettuccine, or any long ribbon variety

Put several quarts of water on to boil. Cut bell peppers lengthwise into quarters. Remove the seeds and pith and slice across each section to create uniform ¼-inch strips. Halve the red peppers lengthwise, remove seeds and pith, and slice crosswise into uniform ¼-inch strips. Melt the butter in a large skillet, add the chili flakes and garlic, and stir a moment before adding the peppers, onion, almonds, salt, and pepper. Stir and toss a minute or two over medium-high heat. The peppers should sizzle and fry in the butter. As the peppers begin to release their liquid you may leave the pan, but continue to stir frequently as they sauté 10 minutes. Meanwhile, cook the pasta until al dente. When peppers are a little limp and well browned, sprinkle on the oregano, turn off the heat, and add the parsley and sherry. Stir the peppers as the liquid sizzles and steams. Toss this mixture with hot, drained noodles, grind on a little more pepper, and garnish the bowl or platter with parsley sprigs. Sprinkle with Parmesan and serve.

Each serving provides:

593	Calories	78 g	Carbohydrate
19 g	Protein	390 mg	Sodium
21 g	Fat	30 mg	Cholesterol

✔ Pizza Pasta

Here, favorite pizza toppings become a quick and delicious sauce for pasta. For best results, use fontina or another good melting cheese.

Yield: 6 main-course servings

Olive oil	4	tablespoons
Onion	1	medium, chopped
Green bell pepper	1	small, chopped
Garlic	2	medium cloves, minced
Mushrooms, chopped	2	cups
Black olives, coarsely chopped	1	cup
Fresh tomatoes	1	pound, chopped
Dried basil	1	teaspoon
Dried oregano	1	teaspoon
Dried thyme		A pinch
Cayenne pepper		A few shakes
Dry red wine	¼	cup
Fontina cheese, grated	1	cup
Parmesan cheese, finely grated	¼	cup
Dried pasta	12	ounces

Recommended pasta: spirals, tubes, or shells

Put several quarts of water on to boil for the pasta. Heat 2 table-spoons of the olive oil in a skillet. Add the onion, bell pepper, and garlic, and sauté over medium heat about 5 minutes. Add the mushrooms, olives, tomatoes, herbs, cayenne, and wine and simmer, uncovered, about 10 minutes. The vegetables should release their juices and cook down just a bit. Meanwhile, cook the pasta until al dente. Drain briefly. Toss the hot noodles in a warm bowl with the remaining 2 tablespoons olive oil and the cheeses, then toss in the vegetable mixture. Serve very hot and pass the pepper grinder, if desired.

Each serving provides:			
444	Calories	51 g	Carbohydrate
15 g	Protein	435 mg	Sodium
20 g	Fat	25 mg	Cholesterol

Spicy Stir-Fried Tofu and Green Beans

This hearty meal in a dish is a delicious and unusual way to enjoy fresh beans.

Yield: 8 main-course servings

Fresh green beans	1	pound
Firm-style tofu	1	pound
Olive oil	3	tablespoons
Dried red chili flakes	½	teaspoon
Onion	1	medium, coarsely chopped
Garlic	4	medium cloves, minced
Soy sauce	5	tablespoons
Red bell pepper	1	small, diced
Mushrooms	½	pound, sliced
Mirin or sweet sherry	3	tablespoons
Lemon juice	2	tablespoons
Dried pasta	1	pound

Recommended pasta: spaghetti or linguine

Trim the green beans and break or cut into 1-inch pieces. Blot the tofu with a tea towel to remove surface water and dice into ½-inch cubes. Put several quarts of water on to boil for the pasta. Heat the olive oil in a high-walled heavy skillet. Add the chili flakes and stir to distribute. Add the onion and garlic and sauté over medium-high heat, stirring often, 5 minutes. Add 1 tablespoon of the soy sauce and stir to distribute before adding the tofu, bell pepper, and mushrooms. The pan should be hot enough so that the tofu begins to sizzle immediately. Sauté, stirring frequently, about 8 minutes, until the liquid released from the tofu is gone and everything is browning. Bring a few inches of water to a boil in a covered pot, insert a steaming rack, and steam the beans 8 minutes. Drain and add to the tofu mixture. Stir and sauté 5 minutes longer. Meanwhile, cook the pasta until al dente. Drain well and transfer to a warm serving bowl. Add the tofu mixture to the pasta and toss. Whisk together the remaining 3 tablespoons soy sauce, the mirin, and the lemon juice in a small bowl. Pour this mixture over the pasta, toss to combine well, and serve very hot.

Each serving provides:

390	Calories	55 g	Carbohydrate
19 g	Protein	660 mg	Sodium
11 g	Fat	0 mg	Cholesterol

Pasta with Pesto, Potatoes, and Green Beans

"Potatoes with pasta?" you ask. Yes, this combination works very well. The green beans add a nice light crunch.

Yield: 4 main-course servings

Olive oil	1	tablespoon
Garlic	2	medium cloves, minced
Stewed tomatoes	1	14.5-ounce can
Fresh green beans	½	pound
Red potato	1	medium
Basil Pesto	½	cup (see page 32)
Single cream	½	cup
Dried pasta	12	ounces

Recommended pasta: penne or other small tubes

Heat the oil in a large high-walled skillet and sauté the garlic a few moments. Add tomatoes and cook over medium-high heat about 12 minutes to reduce the liquid. Meanwhile, trim the green beans and cut into 1-inch pieces. Dice the potato into

½-inch cubes. Put a couple of inches of water into a lidded pot, insert a steamer tray, and bring to a boil. Steam the beans and potato together until tender-crisp, about 6 minutes. Meanwhile, bring several quarts of water to a boil for the pasta. When the sauce is reduced, stir in the pesto and single cream. Heat through. Cook the pasta until al dente; drain well. Toss in a warm bowl with the steamed vegetables and sauce. Serve immediately.

Each serving provides:

632	Calories	90 g	Carbohydrate
21 g	Protein	469 mg	Sodium
23 g	Fat	18 mg	Cholesterol

Stewed Cauliflower and Potato with Cumin

The vegetables stew until they're soft and blend together to create a wonderfully aromatic topping for pasta.

Yield: 6 main-course servings

Butter	3	tablespoons
Cauliflower	1	medium, chopped
Russet potato	1	medium, diced
Onion	1	medium, chopped
Cumin seeds	1	tablespoon
Garlic	2	medium cloves, minced
Salt	½	teaspoon
Pepper		A few grinds
Tomato juice	½	cup
Dry sherry	½	cup
Water	1	cup
Dried oregano	2	teaspoons
Black olives, coarsely chopped	½	cup
Fresh cilantro, minced	¼	cup
Farmhouse Cheddar cheese, grated	1	cup
Dried pasta	1	pound

Recommended pasta: **sturdy tubes or spirals**

Put several quarts of water on to boil for the pasta. Melt the butter in a high-walled skillet and add the cauliflower, potato, onion, cumin, garlic, salt, and pepper. Sauté over medium heat, stirring frequently, 15 minutes. Add the tomato juice, sherry, water, and oregano and bring to a simmer. Reduce heat to low, cover, and simmer 15 minutes. Vegetables will be very soft. Meanwhile, cook the pasta until al dente. Toss the drained hot noodles with the stewed vegetables in a warm bowl, then toss again with the olives, cilantro, and cheese. Serve very hot.

Each serving provides:

500	Calories	70 g	Carbohydrate
17 g	Protein	548 mg	Sodium
15 g	Fat	35 mg	Cholesterol

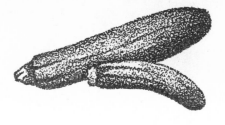

Sweet and Sour Aubergine Sauce

This slightly spicy sauce is one of our favorite ways to eat aubergine, especially served on buckwheat soba, which has a unique earthy flavor. Try it as a main course for a large group of friends.

Yield: 10 main-course servings

Sesame seeds	3	tablespoons
Roasted sesame oil	2	tablespoons
Onion	1	medium, chopped
Garlic	3	medium cloves, minced
Dried red chili flakes	½	teaspoon
Aubergines	2	medium (about 2 pounds), chopped
Yellow or red bell peppers	2	medium, chopped
Tomato puree	½	cup
Ground ginger	1½	teaspoons
Soy sauce	3	tablespoons
Cider vinegar	3	tablespoons
Honey	3	tablespoons
Arrowroot powder	1	tablespoon
Fresh cilantro, minced	½	cup
Dried pasta	1½	pounds

Recommended pasta: buckwheat soba or linguine

Toast the sesame seeds (see page 20) and set aside. Heat the oil and 2 tablespoons water in a high-walled skillet and sauté the onion, garlic, and chili flakes a few moments. Stir in the aubergine and bell peppers. Sauté over low heat about 20 minutes, stirring frequently. The vegetables should become limp but not extremely soft. Meanwhile, bring several quarts of water to a boil. Whisk together 1½ cups water, the tomato puree, ginger, and soy sauce. Add to the skillet and simmer, covered, 10 minutes. Cook pasta until al dente and drain well. (If using buckwheat soba, cook a bit past the al dente stage—until fairly soft, but not mushy.) Whisk the vinegar, honey, and arrowroot powder together in a small bowl. Add the vinegar mixture to the vegetables, turn off heat, and stir and turn a few moments until sauce thickens. Make a bed of the pasta on a platter or in a shallow bowl, arrange aubergine sauce on top, and sprinkle with cilantro and sesame seeds. Serve very hot.

Each serving provides:

351	Calories	66 g	Carbohydrate
11 g	Protein	368 mg	Sodium
5 g	Fat	0 mg	Cholesterol

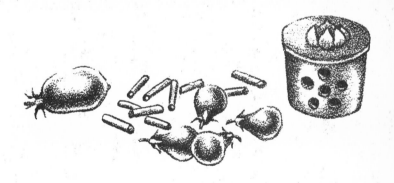

Carrots and Artichoke Hearts with Pistachios and Feta

The delicate but distinctive flavors of the individual ingredients blend well in this Greek-inspired feast.

Yield: 6 main-course servings

Carrots	2	medium
Water-packed artichoke bottoms	1	14-ounce can, drained
Shelled whole pistachios	½	cup
Olive oil	4	tablespoons
Red onion	1	large, coarsely chopped
Garlic	2	medium cloves, minced
Dried red chili flakes	½	teaspoon
Fresh parsley, minced	¼	cup, firmly packed
Lemon juice	2	tablespoons
Water	¼	cup
Feta cheese	4	ounces, crumbled
Lemon wedges	1	per serving
Dried pasta	12	ounces

Recommended pasta: mostaccioli, penne, or spirals

Slice the carrots on the diagonal into ⅛-inch discs. Chop the artichoke bottoms into bite-size wedges. Remove as much of the pistachios' papery skin as you can and toast them (see page 20). Mince the pistachios and set aside. Put several quarts of water on to boil for the pasta. Heat 2 tablespoons of the olive oil in a large skillet. Add the carrots, onion, garlic, and chili flakes and sauté over medium heat about 10 minutes, stirring frequently. Add the artichoke bottoms and parsley and sauté, stirring occasionally, 5 minutes longer. Stir in the lemon juice and water and immediately turn off the heat. Meanwhile, cook the pasta until al dente and drain briefly. In a warm serving dish, toss the hot noodles with the remaining 2 tablespoons olive oil, the feta, and pistachios. Add the sautéed vegetables and toss again. Serve hot with lemon wedges.

Each serving provides:			
452	Calories	57 g	Carbohydrate
15 g	Protein	253 mg	Sodium
19 g	Fat	17 mg	Cholesterol

Mediterranean Asparagus and Artichokes

This was inspired by a day when glorious sunshine fooled us into thinking it was spring. We began to dream of the Mediterranean Sea and invented this dish to take us there in spirit.

Yield: 6 main-course servings

Asparagus	1½	pounds
Marinated artichoke hearts	1	15-ounce jar
Olive oil	4	tablespoons
Onion	1	medium, coarsely chopped
Garlic	4	medium cloves, minced
Dried oregano	2	teaspoons
Dried spearmint	2	teaspoons
Salt	¼	teaspoon
Pepper		A few grinds
Dried tomatoes, slivered	½	cup
White wine	¾	cup
Parmesan cheese, finely grated	½	cup
Fresh parsley, minced	¼	cup
Dried pasta	1	pound

Recommended pasta: sturdy tubes or spirals

Put several quarts of water on to boil for the pasta. Break off the tough stem ends of the asparagus and cut at a slant into 1-inch pieces. Drain the artichoke hearts, reserving the liquid for another use. Heat 2 tablespoons of the olive oil in a large skillet. Sauté the onion and garlic with the oregano and spearmint 5 minutes, until the onion is golden and limp. Add the asparagus, salt, and pepper; stir and sauté 5 minutes. Add the artichoke hearts and dried tomatoes; stir and sauté 5 minutes longer. Meanwhile, cook the pasta until al dente. Drain well. Stir the wine into the asparagus mixture and immediately turn off the heat. In a warm serving bowl, toss the hot drained noodles with the remaining 2 tablespoons olive oil and the Parmesan. Toss again with the vegetable mixture. Sprinkle with the minced parsley and serve.

Each serving provides:

492	Calories	70 g	Carbohydrate
18 g	Protein	302 mg	Sodium
14 g	Fat	6 mg	Cholesterol

Grilled Vegetables in Dried-Tomato Marinade

This dish is best prepared during the summer when you can use the barbecue. The flavors are wonderful, as is the presentation—perfect for an outdoor dinner party. You can grill and marinate the vegetables before your guests arrive, if you wish.

Yield: 6 main-course servings

The marinade

Olive oil	⅓	cup
Balsamic vinegar	2	tablespoons
Lemon juice	1	tablespoon
Garlic	4	medium cloves, minced
Fresh basil leaves, minced	¼	cup
Fresh parsley, minced	½	cup
Fresh thyme leaves, minced	1	tablespoon
Dried tomatoes, chopped	¾	cup
Salt and pepper		To taste

The vegetables

Red onions	2	medium
Zucchini or crookneck squash	4	small
Japanese eggplants	4	small
Belgian endive	2	heads
Olive oil	2	tablespoons
Parmesan cheese, finely grated	¾	cup
Dried pasta	1	pound

Recommended pasta: spirals or spaghetti

The marinade can be made ahead, or just before dinnertime. Whisk together the olive oil, vinegar, and lemon juice until light and slightly creamy in appearance. Add the garlic, basil, parsley, thyme, and dried tomatoes. Stir to combine. Add salt and pepper if desired. Set aside at room temperature.

Heat the grill. Cut the red onions into ½-inch slices. Cut the squash lengthwise into quarters. Halve the eggplants lengthwise. Leave the stem end intact on the endive, but slice it lengthwise and fan it out. Place the vegetables on a large platter and brush them lightly with the olive oil. Since the onions have the longest cooking time and are the least delicate of all the vegetables, place them on the hottest part of the grill. Cook them about 3 minutes, then turn them and continue to cook. Next, place the squash on the grill, then the eggplant and endive. Turn after about 2 minutes. When all the vegetables are tender, transfer them to a large bowl. Allow them to cool slightly, then cut them into small pieces. Pour the marinade over the vegetables and toss well to combine. Marinate about 1 hour at room temperature. When you are ready to serve dinner, bring several quarts of water to a boil and cook the pasta until al dente. Drain well and combine with the vegetables. Toss well to coat with the marinade and to distribute the vegetables throughout. Serve at once, passing the Parmesan.

Each serving provides:

571	Calories	77 g	Carbohydrate
19 g	Protein	260 mg	Sodium
22 g	Fat	10 mg	Cholesterol

Summer Squash with Fresh Basil and Madeira

At the height of summer, pick young squash and mature basil to create this light and refreshing dish. If you combine green zucchini or scallop squash with yellow crookneck, the colors will interplay very nicely on the plate.

Yield: 6 main-course servings

Olive oil	3	tablespoons
Onions	2	medium, chopped
Garlic	3	medium cloves, minced
Summer squash	1½	pounds, coarsely chopped
Salt	½	teaspoon
Cayenne pepper	⅛	teaspoon
Fresh basil leaves	2	cups, loosely packed
Madeira	½	cup
Parmesan cheese, finely grated	½	cup
Eggs	2	large
Lemon wedges	1	per serving
Dried pasta	12	ounces

Recommended pasta: **spaghetti or linguine**

Heat 2 tablespoons of the olive oil in a heavy skillet over medium heat. Sauté the onion and garlic about 3 minutes, until onion is barely translucent. Add the squash, salt, and cayenne pepper; stir and sauté 5 minutes longer. Add 2 tablespoons water, cover tightly, and cook over low heat about 10 minutes.

The squash should be crisp-tender. Add the basil. Stir a moment or two, until the basil begins to wilt. Add the Madeira, bring to a simmer, and turn off the heat. Meanwhile, bring several quarts of water to a boil and cook the pasta until al dente. Drain well. Toss in a warm serving bowl with the Parmesan. Add the squash mixture and toss again. Lightly beat the eggs and add to the bowl, lifting and turning the pasta to distribute the egg evenly.* Act quickly so the eggs do not cook, but rather are incorporated into the sauce. Serve very hot with lemon wedges and additional Parmesan, if you wish.

Each serving provides:

413	Calories	57 g	Carbohydrate
15 g	Protein	366 mg	Sodium
12 g	Fat	77 mg	Cholesterol

---

*Due to the controversy concerning raw eggs and salmonella bacteria, add eggs when the sauce is very hot, *not* warm.

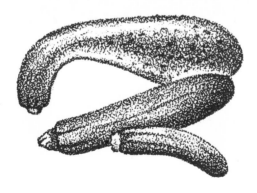

Spinach and Aubergine with Dried Tomato and Feta

Cooking the fresh spinach separately and very briefly retains its bright flavor, which is an important part of the pleasure of this dish. Wait to try this until you find spinach at the market that is absolutely beautiful.

Yield: 6 main-course servings

Fresh spinach	1	bunch (about ¾ pound)
Aubergine	2	small (about 1½ pounds)
Olive oil	5	tablespoons
Garlic	3	medium cloves, minced
Dried rosemary	1	teaspoon
Salt	½	teaspoon
Dried tomatoes, slivered	¼	cup, loosely packed
Capers, drained, minced	1	tablespoon
Parmesan cheese, finely grated	½	cup
Feta cheese	8	ounces, crumbled
Lemon juice	2	tablespoons
Pepper		Several grinds
Lemon wedges	1	per serving
Dried pasta	12	ounces

Recommended pasta: vermicelli or linguine

Put a few cups of water on to boil in your pasta pot. Carefully wash the spinach and discard stems. When the water is boiling, drop the spinach into the pot all at once. Cook 2 minutes, or until spinach wilts. Use a skimmer to lift the spinach out of the pot. Cool in a bowl of cold water and use your hands to squeeze out almost all the liquid. Coarsely chop the spinach and set aside. Add a few quarts of water to the spinach cooking liquid and bring to a boil for the pasta. Without peeling, coarsely chop the aubergine. Heat 3 tablespoons of the olive oil in a wok or large skillet. Add the garlic and rosemary, stir and sauté a minute, then add the aubergine and salt. Quickly stir and toss to coat with seasonings. Sauté over medium heat 15 minutes, stirring frequently. It will soften considerably. Add the tomatoes, capers, and chopped spinach, stir to combine, cover, and turn off heat. Cook the pasta until al dente, drain it briefly, then toss in a warm serving bowl with the remaining 2 tablespoons olive oil, the Parmesan, feta, and lemon juice. Add the aubergine mixture, grind in some pepper, and toss again. Serve very hot or at room temperature with lemon wedges and additional Parmesan, if desired.

Each serving provides:

502	Calories	57 g	Carbohydrate
19 g	Protein	840 mg	Sodium
23 g	Fat	40 mg	Cholesterol

Spicy Brussels Sprouts with Baby Corn and Shiitake

This dish packs a hefty wallop on the spicy scale, thanks to a generous quantity of dried red chili flakes. You can reduce the amount, if you wish, or wait to make it until you're in the mood for hot food.

Yield: 6 main-course servings

Dried shiitake mushrooms	1	ounce
Sesame seeds	2	tablespoons
Raw sunflower seeds	¼	cup
Brussels sprouts	1	pound
Carrot	1	large
Roasted sesame oil	3	tablespoons
Garlic	3	medium cloves, minced
Dried red chili flakes	1	teaspoon
Onion	1	large, coarsely chopped
Salt	¼	teaspoon
Soy sauce	3	tablespoons
Water-packed baby corn	1	15-ounce can, drained
Arrowroot powder	1	tablespoon
Dried pasta	1	pound

Recommended pasta: linguine or vermicelli

Soak the mushrooms in 3 cups hot water 30–45 minutes. Lift them from the water, squeeze out excess water, and wash carefully under a thin stream of running water to remove any grit lodged in the layers of membrane under the caps. Cut out and discard the tough stems and sliver the caps. Set aside. Strain the mushroom soaking liquid through a paper coffee filter and set aside. Toast the sesame and sunflower seeds separately (see page 20). Combine the toasted seeds and set aside. Put several quarts of water on to boil for the pasta. Trim outer leaves from the brussels sprouts. If they are tiny, cut them in half. Quarter the larger ones. Cut the carrot into thick 2-inch-long matchsticks. Heat the oil in a heavy high-walled skillet and sauté the garlic and chili flakes for a few moments before adding the brussels sprouts, carrot, and onion. Add the salt. Stir and sauté over medium heat 10–15 minutes, until vegetables are browned and tender. Meanwhile, cook the pasta until al dente. Add the mushroom soaking liquid and soy sauce to the vegetable mixture, then stir in the corn and mushrooms. Heat to simmering. Meanwhile, whisk the arrowroot powder with ⅓ cup cold water. Add all at once to the simmering skillet and stir to distribute. Cook 30 seconds. The sauce will thicken slightly. Toss the hot sauce with the drained pasta in a warmed serving bowl. Garnish with toasted seeds.

Each serving provides:

481	Calories	77 g	Carbohydrate
17 g	Protein	641 mg	Sodium
13 g	Fat	0 mg	Cholesterol

Hot Baba Ghanoush with Pasta

Why not take a favorite Middle Eastern aubergine and tahini dish, usually served as an appetizer, and toss it with noodles to make a complete meal? The results are delicious. Make the sauce several hours before dinnertime so the flavors can blend.

Yield: 6 main-course servings

Aubergine	1	medium (about 1 pound)
Plain lowfat yogurt	½	cup
Tahini (sesame butter)	¼	cup
Dry sherry	¼	cup
Lemon juice	¼	cup
Garlic	3	medium cloves, minced
Olive oil	3	tablespoons
Salt	½	teaspoon
Cayenne pepper	⅛	teaspoon
Parmesan cheese, finely grated	⅓	cup
Fresh parsley, minced	¼	cup
Dried pasta	1	pound

Recommended pasta: spirals or wide ribbons

Heat the oven to 400 degrees F. Pierce the aubergine with a fork in several places and bake in a glass baking dish 40–50 minutes, until it is totally soft and ready to collapse. Prod it with a fork to tell when it is done. Meanwhile, whisk together the yogurt, tahini, sherry, lemon juice, garlic, 2 tablespoons of the olive oil, the salt, and cayenne. Set aside. When aubergine is soft, remove from the oven. When it is cool enough to handle, remove the skin and scoop the flesh into the yogurt mixture. Whip with a fork until homogenous. This much can be done several hours, or even a day or two, in advance. Cover the mixture and refrigerate until you are ready for it.

Bring several quarts of water to a boil and cook the pasta until al dente. Drain well. Meanwhile, heat the aubergine mixture over a low heat on top of the stove just to warm it a bit. Toss the hot, drained noodles with the remaining 1 tablespoon olive oil and the Parmesan. When well combined, add the aubergine mixture and toss again to distribute evenly. Garnish with minced parsley. Serve hot or at room temperature.

Each serving provides:			
473	Calories	67 g	Carbohydrate
15 g	Protein	319 mg	Sodium
15 g	Fat	5 mg	Cholesterol

Tempeh and Veggies with Miso Tahini Sauce

Typically, rich and chunky sauces combine best with a substantial noodle like rigatoni or spirals. But in this case—maybe because of the light touch of lemon—humble spaghetti is the best choice. For a super-quick and simple meal, use lightly steamed instead of sautéed vegetables.

Yield: 6 main-course servings

Aubergines	2	medium
Tempeh	8	ounces
Olive oil	2	tablespoons
Garlic	3	medium cloves, minced
Dried red chili flakes	½	teaspoon
Onion	1	medium, coarsely chopped
Red bell pepper	1	small, slivered
Dried oregano	2	teaspoons
Salt	½	teaspoon
Lemon juice	½	cup
Water	¾	cup
Miso	2	tablespoons
Tahini (sesame butter)	½	cup
Dry sherry	2	tablespoons
Soy sauce	1	tablespoon
Carrots	2	medium, thinly sliced
Cauliflower florets	2	cups
Broccoli florets	2	cups

| Lemon wedges | 1 | per serving |
| Dried pasta | 1 | pound |

Recommended pasta: spaghetti or linguine

Without peeling them, thickly slice the aubergines crosswise at a slant. Dice the tempeh. Put several quarts of water on to boil. Heat the olive oil in a heavy high-walled skillet. Sauté the garlic and chili flakes a moment or two, then add the aubergine, tempeh, onion, and bell pepper. Stir in the oregano and salt. Sauté over medium-high heat 15 minutes, stirring very frequently. The vegetables should brown and fry a bit and become very tender. Set aside.

Combine the lemon juice with the water. With a wooden spoon, mash the miso and tahini together in a small saucepan until homogenous. Pour in about a quarter of the lemon water and whisk to incorporate. Add the remaining lemon water, the sherry, and the soy sauce and whisk briskly until very smooth. The sauce will be thin. Heat this mixture over low heat until hot, but do not simmer. Cook the pasta until al dente, adding the carrots, cauliflower, and broccoli to the pot for the last 4 minutes of cooking time. Drain the pasta and vegetables. Combine in a warm bowl with the miso tahini sauce and top with the sautéed vegetables. Serve very hot with lemon wedges.

Each serving provides:

599	Calories	84 g	Carbohydrate
25 g	Protein	628 mg	Sodium
20 g	Fat	0 mg	Cholesterol

✔ Broccoli-Mushroom Satay

This dish will surprise you with many new flavors. It is easy to prepare and pretty to serve. Stir-fry sauce is a pungent mixture available at Asian markets or gourmet food shops.

Yield: 4 main-course servings

Roasted sesame oil	2	tablespoons
Green onions	5,	thinly sliced
Red bell pepper	1	medium, diced
Green bell pepper	1	small, diced
Garlic	4	medium cloves, minced
Fresh ginger, grated	1	tablespoon
Water	½	cup
Stir-fry sauce	2	tablespoons
Rice wine vinegar	1	tablespoon
Soy sauce	2	tablespoons
Creamy peanut butter	2	tablespoons
Broccoli, coarsely chopped	2½	cups
Mushrooms	½	pound, thickly sliced
Light sour cream	½	cup
Fresh Chinese noodles	14	ounces

Alternate pasta: fresh fettuccine or linguine

Heat the oil gently in a wok or large cast-iron skillet. Add the green onions, bell peppers, garlic, and ginger. Sauté over low heat about 5 minutes, stirring often. Pour in the water, the stir-fry sauce, vinegar, and soy sauce. Whisk in the peanut butter. Add the broccoli and mushrooms and increase the heat. Cover and cook over medium heat about 10 minutes; uncover, stir, and continue to cook 5 minutes. Meanwhile, cook the Chinese noodles a bit past the al dente stage—until fairly soft, but not mushy. Stay close to the pot, as fresh noodles cook quickly. (If using a standard pasta variety, cook until al dente.) Drain and transfer them to a warm serving bowl. Turn off the heat under the sauce, add the sour cream, and stir gently. Pour the sauce over the noodles and serve immediately.

Each serving provides:			
377	Calories	59 g	Carbohydrate
15 g	Protein	528 mg	Sodium
10 g	Fat	7 mg	Cholesterol

Sesame Soba with Burdock Root and Carrot

Rick and Cathy Tokubo inspired this dish. For the most authentic results, use one of the Asian noodle varieties—particularly buckwheat soba. Burdock root is available at Asian markets. Pick up the soba, sesame oil, and the mirin while you are there.

Yield: 4 side-dish servings

Burdock root	1	root (about ¼ pound)
Carrot	1	large
Olive oil	1	tablespoon
Roasted sesame oil	1	tablespoon
Dried red chili flakes	½	teaspoon
Fresh ginger, grated	1	tablespoon
Green onions	2,	thinly sliced
Mung bean sprouts	1	cup
Soy sauce	3	teaspoons
Light sour cream	⅓	cup
Mirin or sweet sherry	1	tablespoon
Sesame seeds	1	tablespoon
Lemon wedges	1	per serving
Soba	8	ounces

Alternate noodle: any thin Asian variety

Peel the burdock root, shaving off only the thinnest layer of skin. Have a bowl of ice water standing by. Cut the root into 3-inch sections, then cut each section into slender matchsticks. As you finish cutting each section, drop the slivers into the ice water to minimize darkening. Leave them there until you need them. Cut the carrot into matchsticks about the same size as the burdock. Add to the ice water. Put several quarts of water on to boil for the noodles. Heat the oils and chili flakes in a heavy skillet a moment. Drain the carrot and burdock and blot them dry with a tea towel, then sauté in the oil over medium-high heat 10 minutes, stirring frequently. They will begin to brown. Add the ginger, green onions, bean sprouts, and 2 teaspoons of the soy sauce. Stir and sauté another 10 minutes while you cook the noodles a bit past the al dente stage until fairly soft, but not mushy. Meanwhile, whisk the sour cream with the mirin and the remaining teaspoon of soy sauce. Set aside. Toast the sesame seeds (see page 20). When the noodles are cooked, drain briefly and toss with the sour cream sauce, then with the vegetable mixture. Serve with lemon wedges in a bowl or on a platter, hot or at room temperature, sprinkled with the toasted sesame seeds.

Each serving provides:			
361	Calories	57 g	Carbohydrate
11 g	Protein	300 mg	Sodium
10 g	Fat	0 mg	Cholesterol

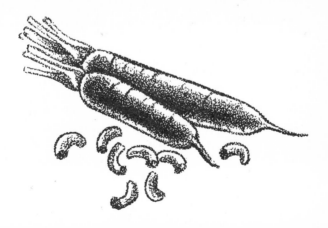

Spicy Greens with Adzuki Beans and Shiitake

Adzukis are tiny, red, protein-packed beans from the Orient. They are available in most Asian markets and natural food stores. For a Far East feast, begin the meal with a very simple miso broth and end with tea and almond cookies.

Yield: 6 main-course servings

Dried adzuki beans	1 cup
Dried red chili flakes	1 teaspoon
Bay leaves	2
Dried shiitake mushrooms	1 ounce
Hot water	2 cups
Mustard greens	2 bunches (about 1½ pounds)
Roasted sesame oil	2 tablespoons
Garlic	3 medium cloves, minced
Onion	1 medium, diced
Fresh ginger, grated	2 tablespoons
Soy sauce	2 tablespoons
Dried pasta	1 pound

Recommended pasta: linguine or lasagnette

Soak the beans several hours or overnight. Drain and cover with fresh water in a large stockpot. Add the chili flakes and bay leaves. Bring to a boil and cook, adding water occasionally as needed, 40 minutes. Beans should be tender but not so soft they break apart easily. Drain the beans and set aside.

Meanwhile, soak the mushrooms in the hot water about 45 minutes. Lift them out of the water, reserving the soaking liquid, and wash carefully under a thin stream of running water to remove any grit in the membranes. Remove the tough stems and sliver the caps. Drain the soaking liquid through a paper coffee filter into a bowl. You will have about 1½ cups, which you will use in the sauce. Set aside.

Wash the greens carefully, discard the thick part of the stems, and chop coarsely. Bring several quarts of water to a boil and cook the pasta until al dente. Meanwhile, in a high-walled skillet or stockpot, heat the oil and sauté the garlic and onion about 5 minutes, until the onion begins to get limp. Add the beans, ginger, and soy sauce, and stir and sauté 5 minutes longer. Add the greens and the mushroom soaking liquid. Toss and stir often as the greens steam and most of the liquid evaporates, about 10 minutes. Gently combine the sauce with the hot noodles in a warm serving bowl. Pass the pepper grinder and additional soy sauce, if desired.

Each serving provides:			
484	Calories	89 g	Carbohydrate
20 g	Protein	378 mg	Sodium
6 g	Fat	0 mg	Cholesterol

Tomato-Based Stovetop Sauces

Tomatoes and pasta are made for each other. When raw or barely cooked, this summer fruit yields a delicate sweetness that perfectly complements pasta's hearty substance. When cooked for a long time, tomatoes are transformed to a thick and rich paste which can stand alone as a sauce or can carry any number of other ingredients.

Many of our recipes call for fresh pear tomatoes. Sometimes called Italian plum or Roma tomatoes, they are small, oblong fruits that have fewer seeds and less juice than salad-variety tomatoes. Their meatier texture reduces quickly to a thick sauce consistency when cooked.

The very best tomatoes are homegrown. Once you have tasted just-picked tomatoes, still warm with the sun, you will understand the difference between truly fresh produce and that which is sold as "fresh" at the supermarket! Tomatoes are simple to grow in areas where the summers are dependably warm and there is ample water for their cultivation.

If you are unable or unwilling to grow tomatoes, seek out a brand of canned tomatoes with a sweet, full-bodied flavor. Stock up on canned whole tomatoes, stewed tomatoes, tomato puree, tomato paste, and pear tomatoes. They will come in handy time after time. Canned tomatoes are not always an appropriate substitute in recipes that call for fresh, but we have offered you the option in several cases.

In this section we explore some of the infinite possibilities suggested by the classic combination of tomato and pasta. We hope they will inspire your own culinary adventures.

Fresh Salsa

We begin this chapter with a simple fresh salsa recipe that can be used in recipes where fresh salsa is called for. If you live in a region where fresh salsa is available from the supermarket, you may want to use the commercial variety instead.

Yield: 5 cups

Fresh tomatoes	2½	pounds
Whole green chilies	1	7-ounce can
Fresh lemon juice	¼	cup
Onion	1	medium, finely diced
Fresh cilantro, minced	⅓	cup
Garlic	3	cloves, minced
Salt	⅛	teaspoon
Black pepper		A few grinds

Blanch and peel the tomatoes (see page 21). Coarsely chop them, drain off as much juice as possible, and set aside in a bowl. Drain the liquid from the canned green chilies. Finely chop them and add to the tomatoes. Add the lemon juice to the tomato mixture, along with the onion, cilantro, garlic, salt, and pepper. Though its flavor improves over time, this salsa can be enjoyed immediately with corn chips or as a topping for Mexican-style dishes. Store the portion you don't need right away in a tightly closed container in the refrigerator for several days, or freeze it for longer periods. If you are accustomed to canning foods, this recipe may be made in larger quantities and put up for the pantry.

Each ½ cup portion provides:

32	Calories	8 g	Carbohydrate
1 g	Protein	158 mg	Sodium
0 g	Fat	0 mg	Cholesterol

✔ Quick and Simple Tomato Coulis

Over the years, you will come up with many tasty variations on this basic theme. If you are having a lot of company, double or triple the amount of tomatoes, garlic, and herbs to increase the yield.

Yield: 4 side-dish servings

Fresh pear tomatoes (or 1 28-ounce can whole tomatoes)	3	pounds
Olive oil	3	tablespoons
Garlic	2	medium cloves, minced
Herbs, fresh or dried		Amounts vary
Salt	½	teaspoon
Pepper		A few grinds
Parmesan or other dry cheese (optional), grated	½	cup
Dried pasta	12	ounces

Recommended pasta: simple strands like spaghetti or vermicelli are traditional with a simple tomato sauce, but you can experiment

Bring several quarts of water to a boil. Blanch, peel, and seed the tomatoes (see page 21), and chop coarsely. If using canned tomatoes, drain off the juice and reserve for another use, such as soup. Heat the oil in a heavy-bottomed skillet and stir and sauté the garlic about a minute, then pour in the tomatoes all at once. Cook over medium-high heat, stirring frequently, about 5 minutes. The tomatoes will break apart and liquefy a bit. Add a tablespoon or so of fresh oregano or basil leaves, or a smaller amount of fresh rosemary or thyme. Any combination of the above is quite appropriate, and delicious. If using dried herbs, begin with a teaspoon or so of oregano and/or basil, perhaps

¼ teaspoon of the stronger-flavored thyme and rosemary. Salt and pepper the sauce at this stage, using the recommended amounts as a rule of thumb, but varying to your own taste. Simmer only a few minutes more over medium-high heat, until the liquid has reduced considerably. You'll know by the look of it when you've achieved the right consistency. The starch from the cooked pasta will thicken the sauce a bit when they are combined, so it's all right for the sauce to appear a bit thin. Meanwhile, cook the pasta until al dente in the reheated tomato-blanching water. In a warmed bowl, toss the tomato sauce with hot pasta and the cheese, if desired. You can pass more cheese at the table. Alternately, you can toss the cooked noodles with a bit of olive oil, portion them out onto serving plates, and top with a ladleful of sauce, sprinkling cheese on top.

Variations: When adding the herbs, you can include a tablespoon or two of capers or chopped olives. A few ounces of red wine, sherry, or brandy can be added for a distinctive effect. In place of plain herbs, you can stir in a few tablespoons of prepared herbal pesto (see pages 31–36). Let your imagination take you for a ride and experiment fearlessly. You might make a delicious mistake!

Each serving provides:

467	Calories	78 g	Carbohydrate
14 g	Protein	304 mg	Sodium
12 g	Fat	0 mg	Cholesterol

Tomato Sauce with Fresh Oregano

Simple tomato sauces can be used in many different recipes. This one has a very fresh, light flavor that works well over noodles or in a baked dish.

Yield: 6 side-dish servings

Olive oil	2	tablespoons
Garlic	3	medium cloves, minced
Whole tomatoes	2	28-ounce cans
Bay leaves	3	
Fresh oregano leaves	¼	cup
Lemon	2	thin slices
Dried pasta	1	pound

Recommended pasta: **spaghetti, linguine, or rigatoni**

Heat the olive oil in a large pan and gently sauté the garlic a few seconds. Add the tomatoes, along with their juice, the bay leaves, oregano, and lemon slices. Cook over medium-high heat about 45 minutes, stirring frequently so the tomatoes do not scorch. The mixture should reduce to a sauce consistency. Meanwhile, bring several quarts of water to a boil and cook the pasta until al dente. Remove the bay leaves and lemon slices from the sauce and serve over pasta, or use in other recipes that call for basic tomato sauce.

Each serving provides:

381	Calories	70 g	Carbohydrate
12 g	Protein	437 mg	Sodium
6 g	Fat	0 mg	Cholesterol

Tomato Pesto Pasta

The pesto gives this tomato sauce a new twist.

Yield: 6 main-course servings

Olive oil	2	tablespoons
Garlic	2	medium cloves, minced
Stewed tomatoes	2	14.5-ounce cans
Basil Pesto	1	cup (see page 32)
Dried pasta	12	ounces

Recommended pasta: vermicelli, spaghetti, or tagliarini

Heat the olive oil in a skillet and sauté the garlic a minute or two. Add the tomatoes and simmer over medium-high heat until liquid is greatly reduced, about 15 minutes. Meanwhile, bring several quarts of water to a boil and cook the pasta until al dente. Drain well and transfer to a warm bowl. Stir the pesto into the tomato mixture and heat through. Toss with the pasta and serve.

Each serving provides:

513	Calories	61 g	Carbohydrate
17 g	Protein	572 mg	Sodium
25 g	Fat	10 mg	Cholesterol

Vegetable Ragout

A good old standby spaghetti sauce—even the carnivores in your family will love it. You can halve or double the quantities for fewer or more diners. Or make a double batch and freeze in quart jars—some hectic evening you'll be glad you stocked up.

Yield: 10 main-course servings

Olive oil	2	tablespoons
Onion	1	large, chopped
Garlic	4	medium cloves, minced
Green bell pepper	1	large, diced
Dried red chili flakes	1	teaspoon
Dried rosemary	1	teaspoon
Mushrooms	½	pound, chopped
Zucchini	2	medium, grated
Dried basil	1	tablespoon
Dried oregano	1	tablespoon
Salt	½	teaspoon
Whole tomatoes	1	28-ounce can
Tomato puree	1	28-ounce can
Bay leaves	2	
Red wine	½	cup
Parmesan cheese, finely grated	½	cup
Dried pasta	2	pounds

Recommended pasta: spaghetti or vermicelli

Heat the olive oil in a high-walled, heavy skillet. Add the onion, garlic, bell pepper, chili flakes, and rosemary. Stir and sauté over medium heat 5 minutes. Add the mushrooms, zucchini, basil, oregano, and salt. Stir and sauté 3 minutes. When the vegetables just begin to release their juices, add the tomatoes, tomato puree, and bay leaves. Bring to a simmer. Reduce heat to low and cook uncovered 20 minutes, stirring frequently. While sauce is cooking, bring several quarts of water to a boil. Cook the pasta until al dente and drain well. Meanwhile, add the wine to the sauce and simmer about 10 minutes. Toss the sauce with the hot pasta and Parmesan. Pass additional Parmesan at the table, if you wish.

Each serving provides:			
464	Calories	85 g	Carbohydrate
17 g	Protein	656 mg	Sodium
6 g	Fat	4 mg	Cholesterol

✔ Angel Hair with Tomatoes and Fresh Basil

This light, refreshing dish is best made in the summer with tomatoes and basil from the garden. However, with fresh basil available in many supermarkets year round, this dish can be prepared in the winter with canned tomatoes. Be sure to heat the serving bowls and the individual bowls or plates. The angel hair pasta is so delicate that it loses its heat rapidly when served in a cold bowl.

Yield: 4 side-dish servings

Fresh pear tomatoes (or 1 14.5-ounce can whole tomatoes)	1½	pounds
Olive oil	2	tablespoons
Garlic	3	medium cloves, minced
Fresh basil leaves, chopped	1	cup, loosely packed
Parmesan cheese, finely grated (optional)	½	cup
Dried angel hair pasta	8	ounces

Recommended pasta: if angel hair (cappellini) is unavailable, substitute vermicelli or thin tagliarini

Bring several quarts of water to a boil. Blanch, peel, and seed the tomatoes (see page 21) and chop coarsely. If using canned tomatoes, drain off the juice and reserve for another use, such as soup. Heat the oil in a large skillet and sauté the garlic a few moments. Add the tomatoes, bring to a rapid simmer, then cook over medium-high heat about 10 minutes, until the tomato liquid is reduced and beginning to thicken. Stir frequently during the last 5 minutes of cooking to prevent scorching. Meanwhile, cook the pasta in the reheated tomato-blanching water until al dente. Drain and transfer to a warm bowl. Add the basil to the tomato sauce and stir to distribute. Pour over the pasta, toss, and serve immediately. Pass the Parmesan, if desired.

Each serving provides:			
315	Calories	53 g	Carbohydrate
9 g	Protein	18 mg	Sodium
8 g	Fat	0 mg	Cholesterol

✔ Pasta Oliveto

You must use the very best fresh tomatoes for this dish, so wait until summertime to make it. Served hot or at room temperature, it is a light but quite satisfying summer luncheon or supper. Crusty French rolls and a crisp green salad would be the perfect accompaniments.

Yield: 6 main-course servings

Fresh tomatoes	3	pounds
Salt	½	teaspoon
Red wine vinegar	3	tablespoons
Pepper		A few grinds
Whole pitted black olives	1½	cups
Olive oil	⅓	cup plus 2 tablespoons
Garlic	3	medium cloves, chopped
Parmesan cheese, finely grated	½	cup
Dried pasta	1	pound

Recommended pasta: **spaghettini, tagliarini, or vermicelli**

Bring several quarts of water to a boil. Blanch, peel, and seed the tomatoes (see page 21) and coarsely chop. In a large bowl, toss the tomatoes with the salt, vinegar, and pepper. Set aside. Drain the olives. In a food processor, puree the olives with the ⅓ cup olive oil and the chopped garlic. Meanwhile, cook the pasta until al dente in the reheated tomato-blanching water. If you wish to serve the dish at room temperature, cool the noodles in a bowl of cold water, drain, and toss with 2 tablespoons of the olive oil. If serving the dish hot, drain the noodles. Toss the hot or cool noodles, first with the olive paste, then with the tomatoes, until everything is well combined. Serve hot or at room temperature and pass the Parmesan and the pepper grinder.

Each serving provides:

535	Calories	66 g	Carbohydrate
15 g	Protein	646 mg	Sodium
24 g	Fat	6 mg	Cholesterol

✔ Light Tomato Cream with Pesto

Pesto and tomatoes, all dressed up! What a pretty presentation this makes when served on an elegant plate garnished with fresh basil and lemon slices.

Yield: 4 main-course servings

Fresh pear tomatoes	2	pounds
Olive oil	2	tablespoons
Garlic	2	medium cloves, minced
Capers, drained, minced	2	tablespoons
Basil Pesto	¼	cup (see page 32)
Light sour cream	¼	cup
Single cream	2	tablespoons
Pine nuts	¼	cup
Parmesan cheese, finely grated	½	cup
Dried pasta	12	ounces

Recommended pasta: **bowties or fancy shells**

Bring several quarts of water to a boil. Blanch, peel, and seed the tomatoes (see page 21). Chop coarsely. Heat the olive oil in a skillet and sauté the garlic a few moments. Add the tomatoes and simmer over medium-high heat until most of the liquid has been reduced, about 10 minutes. Add the capers, turn off the heat, and cover to keep warm. In a small saucepan, blend together the pesto, sour cream, and single cream. Set aside. Meanwhile, cook the pasta until al dente in the reheated tomato-blanching water, drain, and transfer to a warm serving bowl. Gently heat the pesto mixture over very low heat. When it is quite warm, toss with the hot noodles. Top with the tomatoes and pine nuts. Serve at once, passing the Parmesan.

Each serving provides:

617	Calories	77 g	Carbohydrate
24 g	Protein	463 mg	Sodium
26 g	Fat	16 mg	Cholesterol

✔ Tomato Sauce with Tarragon and Capers

This sauce is lightly cooked to retain the tangy flavors of pickled capers and fresh tarragon.

Yield: 6 main-course servings

Whole tomatoes	1 28-ounce can
Tomato paste	⅓ cup
Capers, drained	⅓ cup
Fresh tarragon leaves	¼ cup, lightly packed
Salt	¼ teaspoon
Olive oil	1 tablespoon
Garlic	3 medium cloves, minced
Romano cheese, finely grated	½ cup
Dried pasta	1 pound

Recommended pasta: spaghettini, tagliarini, or vermicelli

Drain the tomatoes, and save the juice for another use, such as soup. In a blender or food processor, puree the tomatoes, tomato paste, capers, tarragon, and salt. Put several quarts of water on to boil for the pasta. Heat the olive oil in a heavy skillet and sauté the garlic a minute or two. Add the tomato mixture and cook over low heat 10–15 minutes or so, until very hot but not simmering. Meanwhile, cook the pasta until al dente and drain well. Toss with the sauce in a warm bowl. Serve hot with a sprinkling of Romano cheese.

Each serving provides:

379	Calories	66 g	Carbohydrate
14 g	Protein	678 mg	Sodium
7 g	Fat	9 mg	Cholesterol

Tomatoes with Sweet Rosemary Onions

Braising in butter mellows the onions to a delectable sweetness which is complemented by the earthy flavor of dried rosemary. Crumble the rosemary between your palms before adding, so it is well distributed throughout the sauce.

Yield: 6 side-dish servings

Butter	2	**tablespoons**
Olive oil	2	**tablespoons**
Onions	3	**large, coarsely chopped**
Dried rosemary	1½	**teaspoons**
Salt	½	**teaspoon**
Fresh pear tomatoes	4	**pounds**
Pepper		**A few grinds**
Dried pasta	1	**pound**

Recommended pasta: **linguine or fettuccine**

The Best 125 Meatless Pasta Dishes

Heat the butter and olive oil in a heavy skillet. Sauté the onions with the rosemary and ¼ teaspoon of the salt over low heat 30 minutes, stirring occasionally. Bring several quarts of water to a boil. Blanch, peel, and seed the tomatoes (see page 21) and chop coarsely. Add the tomatoes and the remaining ¼ teaspoon salt to the onions. Bring to a rapid simmer over medium-high heat, then reduce to low and simmer gently another 20 minutes, stirring frequently. Meanwhile, cook the pasta until al dente in the reheated tomato-blanching water. Drain. Toss with the sauce in a warm bowl and grind a little pepper on top before serving.

<hr>

Each serving provides:

435	Calories	75 g	Carbohydrate
13 g	Protein	250 mg	Sodium
10 g	Fat	10 mg	Cholesterol

<hr>

✔ Angel Hair with Tomatoes and Fresh Shiitake

The delicate strands of angel hair pasta provide the perfect bed for this tomato mushroom sauce. Though light, this dish is very filling. Fresh shiitake are available in well-stocked gourmet food shops.

Yield: 4 side-dish servings

Stewed tomatoes	1	14.5-ounce can
Olive oil	2	tablespoons
Garlic	3	medium cloves, minced
Onion	1	medium, finely diced
Yellow bell pepper	1	medium, finely diced
Dry red wine	½	cup
Fresh shiitake mushrooms	4	ounces, coarsely chopped
Fresh oregano leaves	1	tablespoon
Dried pasta	8	ounces

Recommended pasta: angel hair (cappellini), vermicelli, or thin tagliarini

Drain the tomatoes, reserving their liquid, and dice. Heat the olive oil in a skillet and gently sauté the garlic, onion, and bell pepper about 2 minutes. Add the wine, mushrooms, oregano, and the tomatoes with their juice. Bring to a rapid simmer over medium-high heat and cook about 5 minutes. Turn down the heat and simmer gently about 6 more minutes. Meanwhile, cook the pasta until al dente. Drain well and transfer to a warm serving bowl. Top with the sauce and serve very hot.

Each serving provides:

321	Calories	54 g	Carbohydrate
9 g	Protein	269 mg	Sodium
8 g	Fat	0 mg	Cholesterol

✔ Pasta Primavera

*This dish uses ingredients straight from your summer garden;
however, any grocery store will also have what you need any time of
the year.*

Yield: 6 main-course servings

Onion	1	large
Aubergine, peeled, diced	2	cups
Zucchini	2	medium, diced
Yellow bell pepper	1	medium, coarsely chopped
Fresh tomatoes	2	large, coarsely chopped
Garlic	3	medium cloves, minced
Tomato juice	1½	cups
Fresh basil leaves, minced	½	cup
Single cream	¼	cup
Parmesan cheese, finely grated	½	cup
Dried pasta	12	ounces

Recommended pasta: fettuccine or linguine

Cut the onion in half lengthwise and slice the halves. Combine
with the aubergine, zucchini, bell pepper, tomatoes, and garlic
in a large cast-iron skillet. Add the tomato juice and bring to a
gentle simmer over medium heat. Cover and cook about 10

minutes. Uncover, add the basil, and cook several more minutes to reduce the liquid. The vegetables should be tender but not too soft. Meanwhile, bring several quarts of water to a boil and cook the pasta until al dente. Drain. Just before serving, gently stir the single cream into the vegetable mixture. Spoon the vegetable mixture over the noodles on a warm platter and serve immediately. Pass the Parmesan.

Each serving provides:

314	Calories	55 g	Carbohydrate
13 g	Protein	388 mg	Sodium
5 g	Fat	10 mg	Cholesterol

Spicy Tomato Sauce with Arugula and Calamata Olives

This dish is a nice blending of unusual ingredients. As a variation, you could use fresh chopped spinach in place of the arugula.

Yield: 6 side-dish servings

Fresh pear tomatoes (or 1 28-ounce can)	3	pounds
Olive oil	2	tablespoons
Garlic	2	medium cloves, minced
Dried red chili flakes	½	teaspoon
Calamata olives, chopped	½	cup
Arugula, chopped	2	cups
Parmesan cheese, finely grated	1	cup
Dried pasta	12	ounces

Recommended pasta: rigatoni or penne

If you are using fresh tomatoes, bring several quarts of water to a boil. Blanch, peel, and seed the tomatoes (see page 21) and chop coarsely. If using canned tomatoes, drain them and reserve juice for another use, such as soup. Heat the olive oil over low heat in a large cast-iron skillet. Add the garlic and chili flakes and sauté a minute or two. Add the tomatoes and olives, increase the heat, and simmer about 10 minutes, until the sauce is reduced. Cook the pasta until al dente in the reheated tomato-blanching water, drain well, and toss with the arugula in a warm serving bowl. Pour the tomato sauce over and toss to combine. Serve immediately, passing the Parmesan.

Each serving provides:

364	Calories	50 g	Carbohydrate
16 g	Protein	420 mg	Sodium
12 g	Fat	13 mg	Cholesterol

Spicy Tomato Cauliflower Sauce

This dish makes a hearty cold-weather meal and looks beautifully rich on a plate.

Yield: 8 main-course servings

Olive oil	2	tablespoons
Onion	1	medium, coarsely chopped
Green bell pepper	1	medium, coarsely chopped
Garlic	4	medium cloves, minced
Dried red chili flakes	1	teaspoon
Cauliflower	1	medium
Salt	½	teaspoon
Tomato puree	1	28-ounce can
Dried oregano	1	tablespoon
Water	½	cup
Dry sherry	½	cup
Romano cheese, finely grated	½	cup
Fresh cilantro, minced	¼	cup
Dried pasta	1	pound

Recommended pasta: rigatoni or other hearty tubes

Heat the oil in a high-walled skillet and sauté the onion, bell pepper, garlic, and chili flakes over medium-high heat 5 minutes, stirring frequently. Meanwhile, cut the cauliflower into medium florets. Add the cauliflower and salt to the sautéed vegetables and toss to combine. Add the tomato puree, oregano, and the water. Cook over medium-high heat until the sauce begins to bubble, then turn the heat to low, cover, and simmer 30 minutes. Just before serving, stir in the sherry and heat through. Meanwhile, bring several quarts of water to a boil and cook the pasta until al dente; drain. Toss with the sauce in a warm bowl, then toss again with Romano and cilantro. Serve very hot and pass the pepper grinder and additional grated cheese, if you wish.

Each serving provides:			
342	Calories	58 g	Carbohydrate
12 g	Protein	604 mg	Sodium
6 g	Fat	5 mg	Cholesterol

Tex-Mex Tofu and Noodles

This is a substantial dish—serve only a tart and leafy salad to finish the meal. This recipe calls for fresh homemade salsa. However, you may substitute commercially prepared fresh salsa, bearing in mind the sodium content will be higher.

Yield: 8 main-course servings

Fresh homemade salsa	1½	cups
Fresh corn (or 1 10-ounce package frozen)	3	medium ears
Firm-style tofu	1	pound
Chard	1	bunch (about ¾ pound)
Whole pitted black olives	1½	cups
Olive oil	2	tablespoons
Red onion	1	medium, coarsely chopped
Garlic	2	medium cloves, minced
Chili powder	1	teaspoon
Dried oregano	1	teaspoon
Whole tomatoes	1	14.5-ounce can
Light sour cream	1	cup
Cheddar or jack cheese, finely grated	½	cup
Fresh cilantro, minced	½	cup
Dried pasta	1	pound

Recommended pasta: rigatoni, spirals, or penne

Prepare fresh salsa (see page 172). Set aside. If using frozen corn, set out to thaw well ahead of time. If using fresh corn, cut the kernels from the cob and set aside. Blot the tofu to remove surface water and dice into bite-size cubes. Wash the chard and remove the stems. Sliver the stems and coarsely chop or tear the leaves. Drain the olives and quarter lengthwise. Put several quarts of water on to boil for the pasta. Heat the oil in a high-walled skillet, and sauté the onion and garlic over medium-high heat about 5 minutes, or until they are limp. Stir in the chili powder and oregano, then immediately add the tofu. Stir and sauté another 5 minutes. Add the corn and chard, and sauté until greens are wilted and almost all the moisture is gone, about 5 minutes. Meanwhile, whir the salsa and tomatoes together in a blender for a few moments to create a thick puree. Stir into the tofu mixture, along with the olives, and heat gently 5 more minutes. Turn off the heat and add the sour cream and cheese to the sauce. Stir until the cheese melts and the sauce is well blended. Meanwhile, cook the pasta until al dente and drain well. Toss in a warm bowl with the sauce and serve piping hot with the cilantro sprinkled on top.

Each serving provides:			
478	Calories	65 g	Carbohydrate
23 g	Protein	480 mg	Sodium
16 g	Fat	7 mg	Cholesterol

Tomato Madeira Sauce with Avocado

The dense and rather mysterious flavor of this sauce is enlivened by the addition of ripe raw avocado just before serving. Grilled fish would be a good accompaniment.

Yield: 6 side-dish servings

Fresh tomatoes	1½	pounds
Avocado, firmly ripe	1	medium
Lemon juice	2	tablespoons
Onion	1	medium
Whole pitted black olives	1½	cups
Whole green chilies	1	3.5-ounce can
Olive oil	¼	cup
Dried oregano	1	teaspoon
Cumin seeds	1	teaspoon
Chili powder	½	teaspoon
Dried rosemary	½	teaspoon
Garlic	4	medium cloves, minced
Madeira	½	cup
Salt	½	teaspoon
Cayenne pepper	¼	teaspoon
Parmesan cheese, finely grated	½	cup
Dried pasta	12	ounces

Recommended pasta: medium tubes or spirals

Bring several quarts of water to a boil. Blanch, peel, and seed the tomatoes (see page 21) and chop coarsely. Meanwhile, cut the avocado in half, remove the pit and peel, and dice the flesh into a small bowl. Toss with the lemon juice and set aside. Cut the onion in half lengthwise, then slice each half thickly. Drain the olives and quarter them. Clean any seeds and membranes out of the chilies and slice them into long narrow strips. Heat the olive oil in a large heavy skillet, add the oregano, cumin seeds, chili powder, and rosemary and stir for a moment to distribute evenly in the oil. Add the onion and garlic and sauté, stirring frequently, 7–8 minutes, until onion begins to get limp. Add the tomatoes, olives, chilies, Madeira, salt, and cayenne. Simmer over medium heat 15 minutes. The sauce will thicken and reduce considerably. Meanwhile, cook the pasta until al dente in the reheated tomato-blanching water. Drain thoroughly, toss in a serving bowl with hot sauce and Parmesan, then very gently with avocado in lemon juice. Serve immediately, passing more cheese if you wish.

Each serving provides:

453	Calories	55 g	Carbohydrate
12 g	Protein	624 mg	Sodium
20 g	Fat	5 mg	Cholesterol

Pasta with Peppers and Tomatoes

This sauce is a beautiful bright red, yet not dominated by a tomato flavor. The red bell peppers add sweetness and the chilies a bit of fire. Make this dish at the end of the summer when the ingredients are the freshest.

Yield: 6 main-course servings

Fresh red chilies	16	medium
Fresh pear tomatoes	5-6	pounds
Olive oil	⅓	cup
Red bell peppers	4	large, coarsely chopped
Garlic	7	medium cloves, minced
Salt and pepper		To taste
Dried pasta	1	pound

Recommended pasta: **linguine or lasagnette**

Roast, peel, and seed the chilies (see page 21); if you enjoy very spicy food, leave some or all of the seeds. Cut the chilies into long, thin strips. When working with these mild chilies, you needn't wear gloves; however, be careful not to rub your eyes, as the pepper juice will burn them. Wash your hands with soap and hot water when you finish. Bring several quarts of water to a boil. Blanch, peel, and seed the tomatoes (see page 21) and chop coarsely. Heat the olive oil over low heat in a large cast-iron skillet. Add the chilies and bell peppers, stirring gently to distribute them evenly in the pan. Cook over medium-low heat about 5 minutes, until the bell peppers become limp. Stir in the garlic and cook 5 minutes. Add the tomatoes, bring to a rapid simmer, and cook about 10 minutes, until most of the liquid is reduced. Add salt and pepper to taste. Meanwhile, cook the pasta until al dente in the reheated tomato-blanching water. Drain well and transfer to a warm serving bowl. Top with the pepper-tomato mixture and serve immediately.

Each serving provides:

528	Calories	89 g	Carbohydrate
16 g	Protein	47 mg	Sodium
14 g	Fat	0 mg	Cholesterol

Mexican Pasta

A delightful combination of color, texture, and flavors, just like Mexico! Enjoy it hot or at room temperature. This recipe calls for fresh homemade salsa. However, you may substitute commercially prepared fresh salsa, bearing in mind the sodium content will be higher.

Yield: 6 main-course servings

Fresh homemade salsa	2	cups
Stewed tomatoes	1	14.5-ounce can
Fresh green beans	1	pound
Raw pumpkin seeds	¼	cup
Garlic powder	¼	teaspoon
Fresh cilantro	1	cup, chopped
Light sour cream	1	cup
Feta cheese	8	ounces, crumbled
Avocado, firmly ripe	1	medium
Dried pasta	1	pound

Recommended pasta: penne or other medium tubes

Prepare fresh salsa (see page 172). Combine the salsa and tomatoes in a large skillet. Bring to a simmer over medium heat. Cook, stirring frequently, until the mixture is reduced to a thick sauce consistency, about 20 minutes. Put several quarts of water on to boil for the pasta. Trim the green beans and cut into 1-inch pieces. Bring a couple of inches of water to a boil in a lidded pot, insert a steaming tray, and steam the beans until just tender. Toast the pumpkin seeds with the garlic powder (see page 20). Cook the pasta until al dente, drain well, and place in a warm bowl. When tomato mixture is reduced add the cilantro and the sour cream. Heat just a moment longer (do not simmer at this stage, as the sour cream will curdle). Pour the sauce over the pasta and toss. Add the feta and toss again. Slice the avocado, arranging the slices in a pretty pattern on top of the pasta. Sprinkle with the toasted pumpkin seeds and serve.

Each serving provides:

574	Calories	79 g	Carbohydrate
22 g	Protein	715 mg	Sodium
21 g	Fat	47 mg	Cholesterol

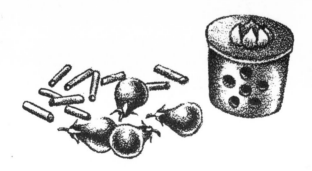

Curried Tomato Sauce with Peanuts and Tempeh

This may sound like an odd combination, but it is delicious and will meet with favorable reviews at your table.

Yield: 8 main-course servings

Tempeh	8	ounces
Butter	4	tablespoons
Garlic	4	medium cloves, minced
Roasted unsalted peanuts	½	cup
Salt	½	teaspoon plus a scant pinch
Onion	1	medium, coarsely chopped
Green bell pepper	1	medium, coarsely chopped
Curry powder	2-3	tablespoons
Whole tomatoes	2	28-ounce cans
Dry sherry	½	cup
Fresh parsley, minced	¼	cup
Dried pasta	1½	pounds

Recommended pasta: spaghetti or linguine

With your hands, crumble the tempeh into very small pieces. Melt 2 tablespoons of the butter in a heavy skillet over medium heat. Sauté 1 minced clove of garlic a moment or two, then add the tempeh, peanuts, and a scant pinch of salt. Stir and brown about 10 minutes. Use a spatula to scrape the bottom of the pan from time to time. The fried tempeh that sticks to it will add a delicious crunchiness to the pasta topping. When it is evenly browned, set the tempeh mixture aside.

Melt the remaining 2 tablespoons butter in a high-walled skillet. Add the remaining 3 minced cloves garlic, the onion, bell pepper, and 2 tablespoons curry powder. Stir and sauté 5 minutes. Pour in the tomatoes with their juice and add ½ teaspoon salt. Bring to a simmer over medium heat, taste the sauce, and add more curry powder if you want a spicier sauce. Reduce heat to low and simmer 20–30 minutes, until a nice thick sauce consistency is achieved. Stir in the sherry and heat through. Meanwhile, bring several quarts of water to a boil and cook the pasta until al dente. Drain well. Toss with the tomato sauce in a warm bowl. Coat the top with the tempeh mixture, then sprinkle with the parsley. Serve hot.

Each serving provides:			
552	Calories	83 g	Carbohydrate
21 g	Protein	547 mg	Sodium
15 g	Fat	16 mg	Cholesterol

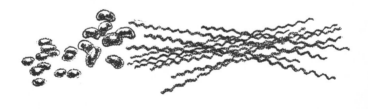

Tomato and Lentil Sauce with Feta

*The lentils add protein and stick-to-your-ribs substance to this dish.
It is hearty enough for big appetites.*

Yield: 8 main-course servings

Dried lentils	1	cup
Whole tomatoes	1	28-ounce can
Onion	1	medium, diced
Garlic	3	medium cloves, minced
Dried oregano	1	tablespoon
Madeira	¼	cup
Black olives, slivered	1	cup
Feta cheese	½	pound
Pepper		A few grinds
Lemon wedges	1	per serving
Dried pasta	1	pound

Recommended pasta: **rigatoni, mostaccioli, or penne**

Carefully sort through the lentils, discarding any tiny rocks you
may find. Rinse the lentils to remove surface dirt, then soak in
a bowl of hot water 2–4 hours. An hour before dinnertime,
pour the tomatoes into a high-walled skillet and add the onion,
garlic, and oregano. Bring to a boil over high heat, then reduce

The Best 125 Meatless Pasta Dishes

heat to medium and simmer until somewhat reduced, about 20 minutes. Add the drained lentils and simmer another 20–30 minutes. Lentils should retain a slight firmness. Stir in the Madeira and turn off the heat. Meanwhile, bring several quarts of water to a boil and cook the pasta until al dente. Drain well. Toss in a warm bowl with the lentil sauce, olives, and feta. Grind a little black pepper on top and garnish with lemon wedges.

Each serving provides:

427	Calories	66 g	Carbohydrate
19 g	Protein	633 mg	Sodium
9 g	Fat	25 mg	Cholesterol

✔ Sauce of Tomatoes, Rosemary, and Garbanzos

This dish makes a wonderful main course, or works well as an accompaniment to grilled fish. The key to this recipe is fresh flat-leaf rosemary. It imparts a less savory, more flowery flavor. The tomatoes can be fresh or canned, depending on the time of year.

Yield: 4 main-course servings

Fresh tomatoes (or 1 28-ounce can whole tomatoes)	3	pounds
Garlic	2	medium cloves, minced
Fresh flat-leaf rosemary	2	tablespoons
Garbanzo beans, cooked	½	cup
Asiago cheese, finely grated	½	cup
Dried pasta	8	ounces

Recommended pasta: rigatoni or other tubes

If using canned tomatoes, drain off the juice and save for another use, such as soup. Chop the tomatoes and combine with the garlic and rosemary in a shallow pan. Simmer over high heat to reduce the liquid, about 10 minutes. Bring several quarts of water to a boil and cook the pasta until al dente. If using canned beans, drain and rinse them. Add the beans to the reduced tomato sauce and heat through. Drain the noodles well and transfer to a heated serving bowl. Toss with the sauce and top with the grated cheese. Serve very hot.

Each serving provides:

311	Calories	55 g	Carbohydrate
14 g	Protein	137 mg	Sodium
4 g	Fat	10 mg	Cholesterol

✔ Brandied Tomato Sauce

This sauce has a unique rich flavor without a bit of alcohol bite.

Yield: 4 main-course servings

Fresh pear tomatoes	2	pounds
Olive oil	2	tablespoons
Garlic	4	medium cloves, minced
Salt	½	teaspoon
Pepper		Several grinds
Brandy	½	cup
Dried pasta	12	ounces

Recommended pasta: **spaghetti, fettuccine, or any thin ribbon or strand**

Bring several quarts of water to a boil. Blanch, peel, and seed the tomatoes (see page 21) and chop coarsely. Heat the olive oil in a skillet, add the garlic, and stir a moment or two over medium-high heat. Add the tomatoes, salt, pepper, and brandy, bring to a rapid simmer, and cook 10–12 minutes, until considerably reduced. Meanwhile, cook the pasta until al dente in the reheated tomato-blanching water. Drain well. Toss the hot noodles with the sauce in a warm bowl and serve immediately, garnished with a bit of chopped parsley if you have some on hand.

Each serving provides:

420	Calories	74 g	Carbohydrate
13 g	Protein	296 mg	Sodium
7 g	Fat	0 mg	Cholesterol

Green Tomato Sauce with Pasta

Many an inspired recipe has come to our tables via the garden. This one makes the best of late-harvest green tomatoes.

Yield: 6 main-course servings

Olive oil	3	tablespoons
Green onions	3	thinly sliced
Garlic	3	medium cloves, minced
Fresh green pear tomatoes	2	pounds (12 medium), diced
Aubergine	1	medium, peeled, diced
Dry sherry	3	tablespoons
Dried tomatoes, minced	¼	cup
Water	½	cup
Dried oregano	1	teaspoon
Fresh parsley, minced	¼	cup
Single cream	2	tablespoons
Parmesan cheese, finely grated	½	cup
Dried pasta	1	pound

Recommended pasta: spirals or bowties

Heat the olive oil in a large skillet and sauté the green onions and garlic about 1 minute. Add the green tomatoes, aubergine, sherry, dried tomatoes, and the water. Cook over medium heat until the green tomatoes are soft, about 20 minutes. Stir often so the tomatoes do not scorch. Meanwhile, bring several quarts of water to a boil and cook the pasta until al dente. Drain well. When the tomatoes are soft, add the oregano and parsley and simmer a few more minutes. Just before serving, stir in the single cream. Place the hot pasta on individual warmed plates and top with the sauce. Pass the cheese.

Each serving provides:

445	Calories	70 g	Carbohydrate
16 g	Protein	186 mg	Sodium
11 g	Fat	8 mg	Cholesterol

Dairy-Based
Stovetop Sauces

Calorie and cholesterol concerns aside, who doesn't love pasta with cream and cheese? For the sake of optimum health, these rather rich dishes shouldn't appear on your table daily. But unless you're on a restricted diet, and on days when your fat intake from other sources has been minimal, you can splurge on a dairy-rich concoction without a twinge of guilt.

    In fact, many of the recipes in this section aren't overly fatty. Although they do all contain some quantity of dairy products, we consistently use lower-fat versions of sour cream, cottage cheese, ricotta cheese, yogurt, and milk. (Do not, however, mistake "imitation" sour cream for a reduced-fat type, as you will be disappointed with the synthetic flavor and consistency.)

If you can't locate these lowfat alternatives in your supermarket, ask your grocer to order them. Or you may prefer the unabashed richness of whole-milk products. Use them, if you wish, with equal success in our recipes.

The most basic cream sauce starts with a roux made by melting butter and stirring in an equivalent amount of flour. This thick paste is stirred and browned just a bit before whisking in warmed milk or cream. The mixture is gently simmered, whisking frequently, until it is thickened and smooth. (The basic proportions are 1 tablespoon each butter and flour to 1 cup milk.) Spices can be heated in the butter before other ingredients are added, or season the finished sauce to your liking. A little salt and pepper are almost always used; from there you are limited only by your imagination.

The assortment of recipes we offer here will introduce you to other simple techniques for dairy-based sauces. Once you learn the basics, be brave and playful and see what new worlds of flavor you can discover.

Leeks, Carrot, and Pecans with Nutmeg Cream

The subtle flavors of pecans and nutmeg bring this beautiful light dish together.

Yield: 6 side-dish servings

Leeks	2	medium (about ¾ pound)
Carrot	1	medium
Butter	3	tablespoons
Flour	1	tablespoon
Salt	½	teaspoon
Freshly grated nutmeg	1	teaspoon
Single cream	1	cup
White wine	¾	cup
Raw pecans, minced	½	cup
Dried pasta	8	ounces

Recommended pasta: spinach angel hair or any thin strand

Trim the root end and most of the green portion from the leeks and discard. Cut leeks in half lengthwise and rinse under cold water to remove any grit lodged between their concentric layers. Blot dry. Cut crosswise at a slant into thin half rounds. Cut the carrot into thin 1-inch matchsticks. Put several quarts of water on to boil for the pasta. Melt the butter in a large skillet, add the leeks and carrot, and sauté over medium-high heat, stirring often, 10 minutes. The vegetables will begin to brown and become limp. Sprinkle with the flour, salt, and nutmeg and stir to distribute evenly. Add the single cream. Reduce heat to low, stir, and simmer 5 minutes. Add the wine and simmer another 5 minutes. The sauce will reduce a bit but will still be a thin consistency. Meanwhile, roast the minced pecans (see page 20). Cook the pasta until al dente and drain well. Just before serving, stir the pecans into the cream sauce, reserving a few for garnish. Gently toss the hot noodles with the sauce and garnish with reserved pecans.

Each serving provides:

334	Calories	38 g	Carbohydrate
8 g	Protein	262 mg	Sodium
15 g	Fat	25 mg	Cholesterol

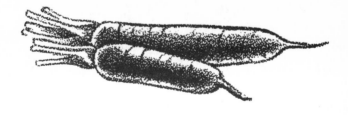

✔ Pasta Carbonara Senza Carne

In classic carbonara style, raw egg is the basis for this rich and flavorful pasta topping. It comes together quickly and will please even the pickiest gourmand.

Yield: 8 side-dish servings

Onions	2	medium
Butter	4	tablespoons
Single cream	½	cup
Egg yolks	3	
Pine nuts	½	cup
Fresh basil leaves, chopped	1	cup, loosely packed
Freshly grated nutmeg	¼	teaspoon
Romano cheese, finely grated	½	cup
Dried pasta	1	pound

Recommended pasta: vermicelli, spaghettini, or any thin strand

Halve the onions lengthwise, then thinly slice the halves. Melt the butter in a large skillet and sauté the onions over very low heat 20 minutes, until very tender. Bring several quarts of water to a boil and cook the pasta until al dente. Meanwhile, in a small saucepan, heat the single cream until barely warm. Just before the pasta is done, beat the egg yolks lightly in a large, barely warm serving bowl. Slowly whisk the warm cream into the egg yolks (if cream is too hot it will scramble the eggs, so let it cool a bit if necessary before proceeding). Stir in the onions. Toast the pine nuts (see page 20). Toss the drained pasta with the sauce until well coated.* Add the basil, nutmeg, cheese, and pine nuts and toss again. Serve immediately on warmed plates.

Each serving provides:

224	Calories	6 g	Carbohydrate
8 g	Protein	171 mg	Sodium
21 g	Fat	141 mg	Cholesterol

---

*Due to the controversy concerning raw eggs and salmonella bacteria, add eggs when the sauce is very hot, *not* warm.

✔ Oyster Mushrooms with Cilantro and Cream

This recipe was inspired by the desire for a light meal following a week of holiday feasting! Look for fresh oyster mushrooms at a well-stocked gourmet or natural food store.

Yield: 4 side-dish servings

Butter	2	tablespoons
Fresh oyster mushrooms	4	ounces, coarsely chopped
Fresh cilantro, minced	2	tablespoons
White wine	3	tablespoons
Dried tomatoes, minced	1	tablespoon
Light sour cream	½	cup
Single cream	¼	cup
Dried pasta	8	ounces

Recommended pasta: penne or other small tubes

Melt the butter in a small skillet and sauté the mushrooms until they release their juice and become limp. Bring several quarts of water to a boil and cook the pasta until al dente. Drain well. Meanwhile, stir the cilantro, wine, dried tomatoes, sour cream, and single cream into the mushrooms. Warm thoroughly over very low heat. Toss the pasta in a warm serving bowl with the mushroom mixture. Serve immediately.

Each serving provides:

339	Calories	49 g	Carbohydrate
11 g	Protein	112 mg	Sodium
10 g	Fat	21 mg	Cholesterol

✔ Light Garlic Cream Sauce

This is quick to make and really delicious. Serve it as a side dish with grilled fish or tofu, if you wish.

Yield: 4 side-dish servings

Butter	2	**tablespoons**
Garlic	3	**medium cloves, minced**
Lowfat milk	½	**cup**
Single cream	½	**cup**
Freshly grated nutmeg	⅛	**teaspoon**
Parmesan cheese, finely grated	½	**cup**
Peas, fresh or frozen	½	**cup**
Dried pasta	8	**ounces**

Recommended pasta: **fettuccine or spirals**

Put several quarts of water on to boil for the pasta. Melt the butter in a small skillet over low heat. Add the garlic and sauté, stirring often, until just beginning to brown. Whisk in the milk and single cream. Add the nutmeg (freshly grated makes all the difference). Cook about 10 minutes over medium-high heat, whisking often. Meanwhile, cook the noodles until al dente. While they are cooking, whisk the Parmesan into the sauce. Stir in the peas and heat through. Toss the cooked noodles in a warm serving bowl with the sauce. Serve immediately.

Each serving provides:

388	Calories	49 g	Carbohydrate
15 g	Protein	319 mg	Sodium
14 g	Fat	37 mg	Cholesterol

Asparagus and Mushrooms in Tarragon Cream

A local Italian restaurant serves a version of this dish during asparagus season. We created our own, lighter version, with the addition of tarragon. It's a perennial hit.

Yield: 6 main-course servings

Asparagus	2	pounds
Butter	2	tablespoons
Garlic	3	medium cloves, minced
Dried tarragon	1	tablespoon
Mushrooms	¾	pound, thickly sliced
Salt	½	teaspoon
Flour	1	tablespoon
Single cream	1½	cups
Freshly grated nutmeg	½	teaspoon
Parmesan cheese, finely grated	½	cup
Pepper		To taste
Lemon wedges	1	per serving
Dried pasta	12	ounces

Recommended pasta: fettuccine or linguine

Break off the tough stem ends of the asparagus stalks, and cut the asparagus at a slant into 3-inch lengths. Melt the butter in a large skillet, add the garlic and tarragon, and stir to distribute. Add the asparagus and mushrooms, sprinkle with the salt, and stir and sauté over medium heat about 10 minutes. Sprinkle the flour over the vegetables and stir to distribute. Add the single cream and nutmeg; reduce heat to low. Bring to a simmer and cook about 5 minutes, until the sauce is slightly thickened. Meanwhile, bring several quarts of water to a boil and cook the pasta until al dente. Toss the well-drained pasta with the sauce in a warm serving bowl. Add the Parmesan and a few grinds of pepper and toss again. Serve immediately, passing additional Parmesan, if desired, and the lemon wedges.

Each serving provides:			
402	Calories	53 g	Carbohydrate
16 g	Protein	406 mg	Sodium
15 g	Fat	39 mg	Cholesterol

Creamy Pasta with Artichokes and Dried Tomatoes

You will enjoy this delicate blending of flavors.

Yield: 4 main-course servings

Pine nuts	2	tablespoons
Olive oil	3	tablespoons
Garlic	2	medium cloves, minced
Flour	2	tablespoons
Lowfat milk	1	cup
Dried tomatoes, chopped	¼	cup
White wine	¼	cup
Dried tarragon	1	teaspoon
Marinated artichoke hearts	1	6-ounce jar
Balsamic vinegar	1	teaspoon
Dried pasta	8	ounces

Recommended pasta: **egg noodles or fettuccine**

Put several quarts of water on to boil for the pasta. Toast the pine nuts (see page 20). Heat the olive oil over low heat in a cast-iron skillet; add the garlic and cook several seconds. Stir in the flour, cooking it about 1 minute to heat through, but not browning. Whisk in the milk, a bit at a time. Continue to cook, whisking often, until mixture is slightly thickened, about 10 minutes. Add the dried tomatoes, wine, and tarragon. Stir often while cooking over low heat about 5 more minutes. Meanwhile, cook the noodles until al dente. Drain well. Just before serving, drain and chop the artichoke hearts, stir them into the sauce, and heat through. Toss the pasta with the sauce in a warm bowl. Add the pine nuts and vinegar, tossing to distribute evenly.

Each serving provides:

430	Calories	55 g	Carbohydrate
13 g	Protein	96 mg	Sodium
18 g	Fat	56 mg	Cholesterol

✔ Basic Alfredo Sauce

Alfredo is the quintessential rich and creamy pasta sauce. Here we present a very basic recipe. It is simply wonderful on its own, or you can top the pasta with steamed vegetables or sautéed mushrooms to create a substantial main course.

Yield: 6 side-dish servings

Single cream	2	cups
Butter	2	tablespoons
Garlic	3	medium cloves, minced
Freshly grated nutmeg	½	teaspoon
Salt	¼	teaspoon
Pepper		To taste
Egg	1	large, lightly beaten
Parmesan cheese, finely grated	1	cup
Dried pasta	12	ounces

Recommended pasta: fettuccine or linguine

Bring several quarts of water to a boil and cook the pasta until al dente. Drain briefly. Meanwhile, warm the single cream in a small saucepan over very low heat. Melt the butter in a high-walled skillet and sauté the garlic over low heat about 3 minutes. Add the warm cream, the nutmeg, salt, and pepper. Continue to cook over low heat until the sauce reaches a simmer. As soon as it begins to bubble, add the pasta and remove from the heat. Push the noodles to the sides of the pan to make a well in the center. Pour the beaten egg into this well and, quickly but carefully, begin to lift and toss the pasta with the sauce until the egg is smoothly incorporated.* Add the Parmesan and continue lifting and tossing until it is smoothly incorporated and everything is well combined. Serve immediately on warm plates, passing more grated cheese and the pepper grinder, if desired. If the pasta seems more gooey than creamy, drizzle on a bit of hot water and toss again, until the right consistency is achieved.

Each serving provides:

438	Calories	47 g	Carbohydrate
18 g	Protein	480 mg	Sodium
20 g	Fat	88 mg	Cholesterol

---

*Due to the controversy concerning raw eggs and salmonella bacteria, add eggs when the sauce is very hot, *not* warm.

Broccoli, Dried Tomato, and Ginger Cream

This unusual combination of flavors will surprise and delight your guests. Serve it on an unusual Asian noodle, like buckwheat soba, to complete the effect.

Yield: 6 main-course servings

Sesame seeds	1 tablespoon
Olive oil	2 tablespoons
Garlic	2 medium cloves, minced
Mushrooms	½ pound, sliced
Onion	1 medium, chopped
Dried tomatoes, slivered	⅓ cup
Salt	¼ teaspoon
Dry sherry	2 tablespoons
Light sour cream	2 cups
Lowfat milk	⅓ cup
Fresh ginger, grated	1 tablespoon
Soy sauce	1 tablespoon
Broccoli, chopped	3 cups, loosely packed
Cayenne pepper	To taste
Dried pasta	12 ounces

Recommended pasta: soba, udon, or any thin strand

Put several quarts of water on to boil for the pasta. Toast the sesame seeds (see page 20). In a large skillet, heat the olive oil and stir in the garlic, mushrooms, onion, and dried tomatoes. Add the salt, stir, and sauté 8 minutes. Turn off the heat and stir in the sherry. In a large bowl, whisk together the sour cream, milk, ginger, and soy sauce, then stir in the sautéed vegetables. Heat gently in a double boiler or place the bowl over the boiling pasta pot. Keep warm. Cook the pasta until al dente, adding broccoli the last 4 minutes of cooking time. Drain well. Toss with the sauce in a warm serving bowl. Sprinkle with the sesame seeds and cayenne, if you enjoy a spicy flavor. Serve on warmed plates.

Each serving provides:			
423	Calories	64 g	Carbohydrate
16 g	Protein	399 mg	Sodium
12 g	Fat	1 mg	Cholesterol

Curried Creamed Eggs

When you're in the mood for comfort food, this rich and creamy curry sauce will fit the bill.

Yield: 8 main-course servings

Peas, fresh or frozen	¾	cup
Eggs	4	large
Lowfat milk	1½	cups
Butter	3	tablespoons
Onion	1	medium, coarsely chopped
Curry powder	1	tablespoon
Flour	3	tablespoons
Salt	½	teaspoon
Carrot	1	medium, thinly sliced
Dried pasta	1	pound

Recommended pasta: spinach ribbons or whole wheat spirals

If using frozen peas, set them out to thaw at room temperature. Hardboil the eggs and cool in very cold water to make the peeling easier. When eggs have cooled, peel them and crumble the yolks into a bowl. Chop the whites coarsely and set aside with the yolks. Warm the milk in a saucepan over very low heat to the scalding point (do not simmer). Put a large pot of water on to boil for the pasta. Melt the butter in a skillet over medium heat. Sauté the onion until it is limp, about 5 minutes. Add curry and flour and stir over very low heat 3 minutes longer. Continue to stir or whisk as you pour in the warm milk. Add the salt. Increase heat to medium. Stir and cook the sauce until it thickens enough to thinly coat a spoon, about 5 minutes. Add the peas and stir a minute longer. Add the eggs and stir gently to distribute them evenly throughout the sauce. Meanwhile, cook the pasta until al dente. Drop the carrot slices into the pasta pot just a minute before the pasta is al dente. Drain well. Arrange cooked pasta with carrots on a platter and pour the sauce over them. Serve very hot.

Each serving provides:			
337	Calories	51 g	Carbohydrate
14 g	Protein	260 mg	Sodium
8 g	Fat	120 mg	Cholesterol

Mushrooms Stroganoff

A recipe we have both been making for years, this mushroom stroganoff is delicious and hearty enough to replace the beef version without any sense of sacrifice.

Yield: 4 main-course servings

Butter	4	tablespoons
Garlic	2	medium cloves, minced
Mushrooms	1½	pounds, thinly sliced
Onion	1	small, coarsely chopped
Water	1	cup
Vegetable broth cube	1	
Flour	2	tablespoons
Tomato paste	1	tablespoon
Light sour cream	½	cup
White wine	2	tablespoons
Dried pasta	12	ounces

Recommended pasta: fettuccine or linguine

Melt 2 tablespoons of the butter in a high-walled skillet, stir in the garlic, then add the mushrooms and onion and stir again. Sauté over low heat until the onion is golden and the mushrooms are limp and have released their juices, about 15 minutes. Meanwhile, heat the water and broth cube in a small saucepan and keep warm. Bring several quarts of water to a boil and cook the pasta until al dente. Drain well. Meanwhile, in a separate skillet, melt the remaining 2 tablespoons butter over medium heat. Add the flour and stir 2 minutes, until it begins to brown. Whisk in the vegetable broth, then the tomato paste. Cook over medium heat, whisking frequently, until sauce is smooth and thickened, about 5 minutes. Turn off heat and stir in the sour cream. Fold in the mushroom mixture and wine. Combine well. Toss with the hot noodles in a warm bowl and serve immediately.

Each serving provides:			
330	Calories	51 g	Carbohydrate
10 g	Protein	126 mg	Sodium
9 g	Fat	21 mg	Cholesterol

✔ Ricotta with Nutmeg and Peas

This dish comes together very quickly, making it a perfect choice when friends drop by and you're in the mood for a light and delicious meal. Serve it with garlic bread and a tart, leafy salad.

Yield: 4 main-course servings

Part-skim ricotta cheese	15	ounces
Butter	4	tablespoons
Peas, fresh or frozen	1½	cups
Freshly grated nutmeg	½	teaspoon
Salt	¼	teaspoon
Pepper		A few grinds
Parmesan cheese, finely grated	½	cup
Dried pasta	12	ounces

Recommended pasta: **small tubes or spirals**

Bring the ricotta and butter to room temperature. Since the sauce will not be heated, you do not want your ingredients to be cold. Bring several quarts of water to a boil and cook the pasta until al dente, adding the peas for the final 2 minutes of cooking time. Meanwhile, mash the ricotta and butter in a bowl with the nutmeg, salt, and pepper. Set the bowl in a warm spot on the stove while you wait for the pasta to cook. Drain the pasta and peas briefly, allowing a bit of water to remain on the noodles. Toss with the ricotta mixture and the Parmesan in a warm bowl. Serve immediately on warmed plates, sprinkled with additional Parmesan and a little nutmeg.

Each serving provides:

669	Calories	78 g	Carbohydrate
31 g	Protein	621 mg	Sodium
25 g	Fat	79 mg	Cholesterol

✔ Savory Ricotta Sauce

This dish is wonderful any time of the year, but especially good on a cold winter night. It has a rich, savory flavor that you will enjoy.

Yield: 6 side-dish servings

Olive oil	¼	cup
Onion	1	medium, diced
Soy sauce	½	teaspoon
Worcestershire sauce	½	teaspoon
Part-skim ricotta cheese	1	pound
Fresh parsley, minced	¼	cup
Fresh basil leaves, chopped	¼	cup
Green onions	2,	minced
Parmesan cheese, finely grated	⅓	cup
Salt and pepper		To taste
Dried pasta	1	pound

Recommended pasta: penne, rigatoni, or other tube

Put several quarts of water on to boil for the pasta. Heat the olive oil in a large skillet. Add the onion and sauté over very low heat until translucent, about 5 minutes. Stir in the soy sauce and Worcestershire sauce, remove from the heat, and set aside. In a saucepan, mix together the ricotta, parsley, basil, green onion, and Parmesan. Stir in the cooked onion. Meanwhile, cook the pasta until al dente. Drain, reserving ⅓ cup of the cooking water, and transfer to a warm serving bowl. Add the cooking water to the ricotta mixture and warm gently over low heat. Toss the sauce with the hot noodles and serve immediately.

Each serving provides:

498	Calories	63 g	Carbohydrate
21 g	Protein	235 mg	Sodium
18 g	Fat	28 mg	Cholesterol

Creamy Red Bell Pepper Sauce with Tarragon

The rather dry texture of ricotta cheese is balanced in this dish by the juicy tang of roasted red bell peppers. Instead of roasting your own, you could buy commercially prepared roasted red bell peppers at a good Italian delicatessen. For this recipe use a cup, drained and chopped.

Yield: 4 side-dish servings

Red bell peppers	2	medium
Butter	2	tablespoons
Garlic	1	medium clove, minced
Dried tarragon	2	teaspoons
Salt	½	teaspoon
Pepper		A few grinds
Part-skim ricotta cheese	1	cup
Plain lowfat yogurt	½	cup
Olive oil	2	tablespoons
Parmesan cheese, finely grated	⅓	cup
Green onions	5	minced
Dried pasta	10	ounces

Recommended pasta: vermicelli or linguine

Roast, peel, and seed the bell peppers (see page 21) and chop coarsely. Put several quarts of water on to boil. Melt the butter in a heavy skillet and sauté the peppers, garlic, tarragon, ¼ teaspoon of the salt, and a few grinds of pepper 10 minutes.

Meanwhile, whisk the ricotta and yogurt with the remaining ¼ teaspoon salt. Cook the pasta until al dente. Add the ricotta mixture to the peppers and stir over low heat until sauce is beginning to simmer, about 5 minutes. Toss hot pasta in a warm bowl with the olive oil and Parmesan, then with the sauce and green onions. Serve immediately.

Each serving provides:			
531	Calories	62 g	Carbohydrate
22 g	Protein	586 mg	Sodium
22 g	Fat	43 mg	Cholesterol

✔ Mushrooms Paprikash

If you can get fresh dill, use it for this recipe. It imparts a wonderfully alive flavor! And be sure to reserve a few sprigs for garnish.

Yield: 4 main-dish servings

Butter	2	tablespoons
Garlic	2	medium cloves, minced
Paprika	1½	tablespoons
Mushrooms	1	pound, thinly sliced
Salt	¼	teaspoon
Light sour cream	2	cups
Prepared horseradish	2	tablespoons
Dill	1	tablespoon dried or 2 tablespoons fresh
Cheddar cheese	4	ounces, grated
Dried pasta	12	ounces

Recommended pasta: fettuccine or linguine

Put several quarts of water on to boil. Melt the butter in a skillet, stir in the garlic and paprika, then add the mushrooms and stir to coat with butter and seasonings. Add the salt and sauté over low heat until the mushrooms release their liquid and it is somewhat reduced, about 7 minutes—only a few tablespoons of the liquid should remain. In a bowl, combine the sour cream, horseradish, and dill. Add this mixture to the cooked mushrooms and stir to combine well. Heat gently about 5 minutes, until sauce is hot (be careful not to heat too rapidly, as the sour cream may curdle). Meanwhile, cook the pasta until al dente and drain well. Toss with the sauce and cheese in a warm bowl, turning gently to distribute evenly. Serve with a sprinkling of dill (or a garnish of fresh dill sprigs) and paprika.

Each serving provides:			
523	Calories	72 g	Carbohydrate
21 g	Protein	390 mg	Sodium
17 g	Fat	45 mg	Cholesterol

✔ Green Chili Sauce with Sour Cream

Canned mild green chilies are the main ingredient in this rich and piquant sauce. It's the kind of sauce that might be served in Mexico if pasta were a staple there.

Yield: 6 side-dish servings

Raw sunflower seeds	3	tablespoons
Olive oil	2	tablespoons
Onion	1	medium, coarsely chopped
Garlic	2	medium cloves, minced
Dried oregano	1	tablespoon
Canned whole green chilies	1	cup, loosely packed
Salt	¼	teaspoon
Black pepper		A few grinds
Red bell pepper	1	medium, grated
Light sour cream	1	cup
Fresh cilantro, minced	¼	cup
Mozzarella cheese, grated	½	cup
Dried pasta	1	pound

Recommended pasta: vermicelli or fettuccine

Put several quarts of water on to boil. Toast the sunflower seeds (see page 20) and set aside. In a heavy skillet, heat the olive oil and sauté the onion and garlic with the oregano 7–10 minutes, until onion is limp and transparent. Place the sautéed onions and garlic, the sunflower seeds, chilies, salt, and black pepper in a food processor or blender jar. Puree until thick and homogenous. Transfer to a saucepan, stir in the grated bell pepper, and bring to the steaming stage over low heat. Combine the sour cream with several tablespoons of the hot chili mixture in a bowl. Stir until smooth. Stir in the cilantro. Add the sour cream mixture to the chili sauce, stir to incorporate, and remove from the heat. Meanwhile, cook the pasta until al dente and drain well. Toss with the sauce and cheese and serve with a sprinkling of cilantro or oregano.

Each serving provides:

452	Calories	67 g	Carbohydrate
16 g	Protein	339 mg	Sodium
14 g	Fat	8 mg	Cholesterol

Spicy Cannellini and Green Beans with Raisins

This unusual blending of ingredients is delicious and protein-packed. It makes a particularly satisfying meal after an active day.

Yield: 4 main-course servings

Dried cannellini or navy beans	½	cup
Fresh green beans	½	pound
Red onion	1	small
Olive oil	2	tablespoons
Garlic	2	medium cloves, minced
Dry sherry	2	tablespoons
Golden raisins	½	cup
Lowfat milk	½	cup
Plain lowfat yogurt	⅔	cup
Light sour cream	½	cup
Curry powder	1-2	tablespoons
Dried tomatoes, diced	¼	cup
Raw walnuts, chopped	¼	cup
Dried red chili flakes	⅛	teaspoon
Dried pasta	8	ounces

Recommended pasta: **penne or other tubes**

Sort and rinse the cannellini beans and soak several hours or overnight. Drain, cover with fresh water in a large pot, and bring to a simmer. Cook uncovered 25 minutes, until just tender. Drain, reserving the liquid for a soup stock or other use. Put several quarts of water on to boil for the pasta. Trim the green beans and cut at a slant into 1-inch pieces. Cut the onion in half lengthwise and thickly slice each half. Heat the olive oil

The Best 125 Meatless Pasta Dishes

in a large skillet and sauté the onion and garlic several minutes, until onion is limp and transparent. Stir in the cooked cannellini beans, the green beans, sherry, and raisins. Stir and sauté 2 minutes longer. In a bowl, stir together the milk, yogurt, sour cream, curry powder, and dried tomato. Add to the skillet, cover, and cook over low heat about 10 minutes, until green beans are tender-crisp. Toast the walnuts with the chili flakes (see page 20). Meanwhile, cook the pasta until al dente and drain well. Toss the pasta with the sauce in a warm bowl. Top with the walnuts and serve immediately.

Each serving provides:

585	Calories	91 g	Carbohydrate
22 g	Protein	107 mg	Sodium
16 g	Fat	3 mg	Cholesterol

Brandied Mushrooms with Two Cheeses

Porcini, Italian field mushrooms, are one of nature's richest-tasting foods. They are too expensive for most of us to enjoy in large quantities; fortunately, a little goes a long way.

Yield: 6 main-course servings

Dried porcini	½	ounce
Fontina cheese	4	ounces
Butter	4	tablespoons
Mushrooms	½	pound, thinly sliced
Flour	2	tablespoons
Lowfat milk	1	cup
Brandy	¼	cup
Salt	½	teaspoon
Parmesan cheese, finely grated	½	cup
Fresh parsley, minced	¼	cup
Freshly grated nutmeg	1	teaspoon
Dried pasta	12	ounces

Recommended pasta: fettuccine, linguine, or any thin ribbon or strand

Soak the porcini in 1 cup warm water about half an hour. Lift the porcini from the water and chop coarsely. Strain the soaking liquid through a paper coffee filter and set aside. Dice the fontina into ¼-inch pieces. Put several quarts of water on to boil for the pasta. Melt the butter and sauté the porcini over medium heat 5 minutes, then add the sliced mushrooms and sauté 10 minutes longer, until they have released their liquid and are limp. Sprinkle on the flour and stir to distribute. Stir in the milk, brandy, and ½ cup of the porcini soaking liquid. Add the salt and simmer the mixture over low heat 5–10 minutes, until slightly thickened. Meanwhile, cook the pasta until al dente and drain well. In a warm bowl, combine the mushroom sauce, the fontina and Parmesan, and the pasta. Gently stir and turn the noodles until the cheese is melted and the sauce is evenly distributed. Garnish with the parsley and nutmeg and serve immediately.

Each serving provides:			
248	Calories	8 g	Carbohydrate
11 g	Protein	587 mg	Sodium
17 g	Fat	51 mg	Cholesterol

✔ Sauce of Feta, Fresh Herbs, and Cashews

For this recipe, it is preferable to put the garlic through a press rather than mincing it with a knife, as you want the garlic to liquefy a bit and distribute well in the oil. If you're using dill or oregano, 2 tablespoons will not be too much. With the woodier rosemary, use only 1 tablespoon.

Yield: 6 side-dish servings

Olive oil	⅓	cup
Garlic	2	medium cloves, pressed
Fresh oregano, dill, or rosemary, minced	1-2	tablespoons
Parmesan cheese, finely grated	⅓	cup
Feta cheese, crumbled	1	cup
Roasted unsalted cashews	1	cup
Lemon wedges	1	per serving
Dried pasta	12	ounces

Recommended pasta: spirals or vermicelli

A few hours before mealtime, stir together the olive oil, garlic, and minced herbs in a small saucepan. Set aside at room temperature so the flavors can blend. When ready to eat, bring several quarts of water to a boil and cook the pasta until al dente. Drain well. Meanwhile, barely heat the olive oil mixture over low heat. In a warm bowl, toss the hot noodles with the oil and Parmesan, then with the feta and cashews. Serve immediately with a lemon wedge on each plate. Pass the pepper grinder, if desired.

Each serving provides:

528	Calories	51 g	Carbohydrate
16 g	Protein	359 mg	Sodium
30 g	Fat	24 mg	Cholesterol

Creamy Aubergine and Gorgonzola Sauce

In this dish, the aubergine is cooked long enough to become a sauce in itself. It blends beautifully with the piquant gorgonzola.

Yield: 8 side-dish servings

Aubergine	2	small (about 1½ pounds)
Chard	1	bunch (about ¾ pound)
Onion	1	medium
Water	½	cup
Raw walnuts, chopped	1	cup
Salt	¼	teaspoon
Fresh basil leaves	1	cup, loosely packed
Olive oil	2	tablespoons
Gorgonzola cheese, crumbled	1	cup
Dried pasta	1	pound

Recommended pasta: **penne or rigatoni**

Choose small, firm aubergines. Without peeling, dice them. Wash chard, remove and sliver the stems, and tear the leaves into pieces. Cut the onion lengthwise in half, then thinly slice each half. Toast the walnuts (see page 20). In a high-walled skillet, heat the water to boiling. Place the aubergine, chard stems, and onion in the water, sprinkle with the salt, and simmer, covered, over low heat 20 minutes. Vegetables will be very soft. Stir in the chard leaves and basil and simmer, uncovered, about 5 minutes, or until liquid is almost gone. Meanwhile, bring several quarts of water to a boil and cook the pasta until al dente. Drain well. Toss with the olive oil, then with the aubergine mixture, then with the cheese and half the walnuts. Serve in a large, shallow bowl garnished with a few basil leaves and the remaining walnuts. Pass the pepper grinder, if desired.

Each serving provides:

431	Calories	53 g	Carbohydrate
15 g	Protein	396 mg	Sodium
19 g	Fat	13 mg	Cholesterol

Blue Cheese Pasta and Veggies

The combination of garlic and blue cheese is intensely rich and aromatic and not for the faint of heart. The simplicity of preparation is an added bonus.

Yield: 8 main-course servings

Broccoli, chopped	3	cups, loosely packed
Carrots	2	medium, thinly sliced
Crookneck squash or zucchini	2	medium, diced
Olive oil	⅓	cup
Butter	3	tablespoons
Garlic	2	medium cloves, minced
Cayenne pepper	¼	teaspoon
Blue cheese	8	ounces, crumbled
Parmesan cheese, finely grated	½	cup
Dried pasta	1	pound

Recommended pasta: linguine, tagliarini, or spaghetti

Put several quarts of water on to boil for the pasta. Use plenty of water, as it must accommodate the vegetables as well. Cook the pasta until al dente, adding the broccoli, carrots, and squash for the last 3 minutes of cooking time. Meanwhile, warm the olive oil, butter, garlic, and cayenne in a small skillet or saucepan over low heat for about 5 minutes. See that the oil heats slowly so the garlic doesn't burn, though it may brown a little. When the pasta and vegetables are al dente, drain thoroughly and drizzle the oil mixture evenly over them in a warm bowl. Toss to distribute, then toss again with the blue cheese and Parmesan. Serve very hot.

Each serving provides:			
482	Calories	49 g	Carbohydrate
18 g	Protein	573 mg	Sodium
24 g	Fat	38 mg	Cholesterol

Paprika Blue Cheese Sauce with Green Beans and Pecans

Just enough blue cheese is used to impart a sharp tang and intriguing aroma. The smoky crunch of the toasted pecans completes the picture perfectly. This is a great way to enjoy tiny new green beans from the garden.

Yield: 8 main-course servings

Slender green beans	1	pound
Butter	2	tablespoons
Garlic	3	medium cloves, minced
Paprika	1	tablespoon
Mushrooms	½	pound, thinly sliced
Red bell pepper	1	small, slivered
Salt	½	teaspoon
Lowfat milk	1½	cups
Flour	1	tablespoon
Blue cheese	¼	pound, crumbled
Pepper		A few grinds
Raw pecan pieces	½	cup
Fresh parsley, minced	¼	cup
Dried pasta	1	pound

Recommended pasta: **sturdy tubes or spirals**

Trim the beans and cut at a slant into 1-inch pieces. Melt the butter in a high-walled skillet over low heat. Add the garlic and paprika and stir a bit. Add the beans, mushrooms, bell pepper, and salt. Stir and sauté 5 minutes, until mushrooms are limp and releasing their juices. Warm the milk in a small saucepan over low heat. Put several quarts of water on to boil for the pasta. Add the flour to the vegetables in the skillet and stir to distribute evenly. Add the warm milk, increase the heat to medium, and bring the sauce to a simmer. Add the blue cheese and pepper, and simmer gently 10 minutes while you cook the pasta until al dente. The sauce will thicken a little, but will have a rather thin consistency. Meanwhile, toast the pecans (see page 20) and chop finely. Stir half the pecans and half the parsley into the sauce. Drain the pasta briefly and toss in a warm bowl with the green bean sauce. Sprinkle the remaining pecans and parsley over the top. Serve very hot.

Each serving provides:			
383	Calories	53 g	Carbohydrate
14 g	Protein	396 mg	Sodium
13 g	Fat	20 mg	Cholesterol

✔ Pasta with Gorgonzola and Parmesan

You can make this dish as a delicious main course for 4 people, or serve it as a starter for 8. Use a spinach pasta for a very pretty presentation.

Yield: 8 side-dish servings

Butter	3	tablespoons
Garlic	2	medium cloves, minced
Gorgonzola cheese	4	ounces, crumbled
Lowfat milk	½	cup
Double cream	⅓	cup
Parmesan cheese, finely grated	¾	cup
Dried pasta	1	pound

Recommended pasta: **spinach fettuccine, lasagnette, or tagliatelle**

Put several quarts of water on to boil for the pasta. Melt the butter in a large skillet and stir in the garlic. Heat just a bit, then add the Gorgonzola and milk; stir until smooth. Blend in the cream and just heat through. Cook the pasta until al dente, drain well, and add to the sauce in the skillet. Lift and toss gently to coat, then mix in the Parmesan. Transfer to a warm bowl and serve immediately.

Each serving provides:

382	Calories	44 g	Carbohydrate
15 g	Protein	444 mg	Sodium
16 g	Fat	44 mg	Cholesterol

Baked and Stuffed Pasta

The appeal of casseroles is universal. Nearly every cuisine around the globe has developed unique dishes that are sauced and baked in the oven. In America—as in many other parts of the world—the classic casserole includes noodles and cheese. On this simple foundation, wonderful culinary masterpieces can be built.

A pretty and practical collection of baking dishes will inspire your efforts in this direction. Ovals, rectangles, and squares are the most commonly used shapes, though fun and unusual casseroles can be created in loaf tins or other molds.

There are a few hard and fast rules. Do preheat the oven so the casserole comes up to baking temperature quickly. Use a large pot with plenty of water to cook lasagna noodles. Be sure to include sufficient sauce so the finished product isn't dry and flavorless. Dishes that go into the oven with a cover on will have a uniform tender texture. To create a crunchy crust on top, remove the lid toward the end of the cooking time and let the casserole brown a bit. Allow casseroles to rest at room temperature 10–15 minutes so they can firm up before serving.

Many pasta cooks prefer to make sheets of dough from scratch for casseroles. If you don't wish to spend the time, dried lasagna and manicotti noodles are quite adequate. Try the homemade version some rainy Saturday when pottering in the kitchen feels just right.

As marvelous as they are when hot from the oven, casseroles magically improve with time. Store leftover casseroles covered in the refrigerator. Small amounts can be quickly reheated in a microwave or top oven for a delicious reprise. Many casseroles won't even require reheating—they can be enjoyed the following day at room temperature, or even cold. It's a matter of taste. You can also freeze most casseroles, whole or in individual servings, for a quick meal later.

Fillings for stuffed noodle preparations should be of a thick paste consistency; too runny and the pasta wrapper can become soggy during boiling. Again, you may wish to make fresh dough for stuffing, but fresh store-bought wonton wrappers make delicious ravioli. Look for them in the produce section of your supermarket or at Asian food stores.

A few of the recipes in this section start with commercially prepared stuffed pastas, such as tortellini and ravioli. Try a few different brands to discover the ones you like best. Keep some in the pantry or freezer for a quick pasta feast when time doesn't allow for from-scratch preparations.

Here we present our favorite baked and stuffed pastas. We hope they inspire you to create delectable new classics in your own kitchen.

The Best 125 Meatless Pasta Dishes

Burnt Butter and Wine Sauce for Ravioli

Guy Hadler perfected this wonderfully simple dish. Use commercially prepared cheese ravioli or tortellini when an instant dinner is called for.

Yield: 4 side-dish servings

Butter	3	**tablespoons**
Garlic powder	1	**teaspoon**
White wine	1	**tablespoon**
Lemon juice	½	**teaspoon**
Fresh cheese ravioli or tortellini	8	**ounces**

Put several quarts of water on to boil for the ravioli. Meanwhile, melt the butter in a small cast-iron skillet over low heat. Add the garlic powder, wine, and lemon juice, turn off the heat, cover, and set aside. Cook the ravioli until tender, drain, and transfer to a warm serving bowl. Keep warm. Heat the butter mixture over high heat until it scorches, then turn the heat down to medium-high and reduce for a minute or two before drizzling it evenly over the ravioli. Serve immediately.

Each serving provides:

261	Calories	17 g	Carbohydrate
9 g	Protein	373 mg	Sodium
17 g	Fat	70 mg	Cholesterol

Spinach Aubergine Lasagna

This Mediterranean-style lasagna has a wonderful flavor, light and fresh. And the layers create a beautiful color palette. As a variation, prepare it well ahead of time, let it cool, and serve small portions as appetizers.

Yield: 10 main-course servings

The sauce

Olive oil	2	tablespoons
Garlic	2	medium cloves, minced
Onion	1	medium, finely diced
Stewed tomatoes	1	28-ounce can
Lemon	2	slices
Bay leaves	3	
Fresh basil leaves, minced	3	tablespoons

The casserole

Fresh spinach	1	bunch (about ¾ pound)
Aubergine	1	medium (about 1 pound)
Olive oil	4	tablespoons
Firm-style tofu	¾	pound
Part-skim ricotta cheese	2½	cups
Garlic	3	medium cloves, minced
Part-skim mozzarella cheese	1	pound, shredded
Green onions	6	sliced
Parmesan cheese, finely grated	⅓	cup
Dried lasagna noodles	12	ounces

Preheat the oven to 350 degrees F. about 30 minutes before you are ready to bake the lasagna. To prepare the sauce, heat 2 tablespoons olive oil in a large pan and sauté the garlic and onion a couple of minutes. Add the tomatoes, lemon slices, bay leaves, and basil. Cook the sauce about 30 minutes, until it reduces slightly. Remove the lemon slices and bay leaves. Set aside.

Meanwhile, bring several quarts of water to a boil and cook the noodles until almost al dente. They will finish cooking in the oven. Cool the noodles in a large bowl of cold water that has a tablespoon of olive oil added. Drain and lay them on a tea towel to dry. Carefully wash the spinach, remove the stems, and place the leaves in a steamer rack over a couple of inches of boiling water in a lidded pot. Steam until it wilts. Place the cooked spinach in a colander to drain. Peel the aubergine and cut lengthwise into ½-inch-thick slices. Heat a little olive oil in a cast-iron skillet over medium heat and sauté the aubergine slices about 2 minutes per side until tender. This will need to be done in several batches, adding a little more olive oil each time (but don't exceed a total of 2 tablespoons of oil). Drain the cooked aubergine on paper towels until needed. Slice the tofu and blot with a tea towel to remove surface water. Mash it in a bowl with a potato masher or fork. Mix in the ricotta and garlic. Rub an 11 × 14-inch baking dish with 1 tablespoon olive oil. (If you do not have a dish this size you will have extra noodles, so hold out some of the other ingredients, which can be layered in a bread pan to create a second small casserole.) Layer the casserole as follows:

half the tomato sauce
layer of noodles
all the aubergine slices
¾ of the mozzarella
layer of noodles

remainder of tomato sauce

ricotta-tofu mixture

spinach

green onions

remainder of mozzarella

Parmesan

Cover and bake 30–40 minutes. Let stand 15 minutes before serving.

Each serving provides:

534	Calories	39 g	Carbohydrate
33 g	Protein	546 mg	Sodium
27 g	Fat	48 mg	Cholesterol

Pasta al Pesto Frittata

This unusual egg and pasta casserole comes together quickly. Serve it for brunch, lunch, or dinner, accompanied by a tangy salad or steamed vegetables.

Yield: 8 side-dish servings

Olive oil	1	tablespoon
Eggs	6	large
Basil Pesto	¼	cup (see page 32)
Salt		A scant pinch
Pepper		A few grinds
Part-skim mozzarella cheese, shredded	¾	cup
Dried pasta	6	ounces

Recommended pasta: **linguine or spaghetti**

Put a few quarts of water on to boil for the pasta. Preheat the oven to 375 degrees F. Rub the olive oil onto a heavy 10-inch skillet that can take the heat of the oven. Cook the pasta until al dente. Drain well. Distribute it in an even thickness over the bottom of the skillet and allow to cool 10 minutes. Meanwhile, whisk the eggs with the pesto, salt, and pepper, then stir in the cheese. Pour the egg mixture over the pasta, again being careful to distribute evenly. Bake uncovered 20 minutes, cut in wedges, and serve hot or at room temperature.

Each serving provides:

209	Calories	18 g	Carbohydrate
12 g	Protein	158 mg	Sodium
10 g	Fat	167 mg	Cholesterol

Mexicali Lasagna

Some traditional tamale pie ingredients are combined here to create a very unusual lasagna. It has been enjoyed by many friends, who were delightfully surprised by the green chilies and corn.

Yield: 8 main-course servings

The sauce

V-8 juice	2	cups
Lowfat milk	1	cup
Fresh cilantro, minced	⅓	cup, loosely packed
Dried oregano	1	tablespoon
Garlic powder	1	teaspoon
Flour	¼	cup

The casserole

Broccoli florets	2	cups, loosely packed
Canned whole green chilies	1½	cups, loosely packed
Olive oil	1	tablespoon
Part-skim ricotta cheese	15	ounces
Farmhouse Cheddar cheese	8	ounces, shredded
Frozen corn	1	10-ounce package
Parmesan cheese, finely grated	2	tablespoons
Dried lasagna noodles	8	ounces

Well ahead of time, set the frozen corn out to thaw. Preheat the oven to 375 degrees F. about 30 minutes before you are ready to bake the lasagna. In a medium-size saucepan, heat the V-8 juice, milk, cilantro, oregano, and garlic powder. When this mixture is steaming hot, shake the flour in a small jar with ⅓ cup water until flour is incorporated. Whisk this roux into the sauce and simmer over low heat, whisking frequently, until slightly thickened, about 10 minutes.

Meanwhile, bring several quarts of water to a boil and cook noodles until almost tender. They will finish cooking in the oven. During the last 5 minutes of pasta cooking time, add the broccoli florets to the pot. Cool in cold water and drain, then lay noodles out in a single layer on a tea towel until needed. Set the broccoli aside. Clean the seeds and membranes from the chilies and slice into thin strips. Rub a 9 × 13-inch baking dish with 1 tablespoon olive oil. Ladle ½ cup sauce into the bottom and distribute evenly. Place a single layer of noodles over the sauce. Use half the chili strips to make a layer on top of the noodles. Use a soup spoon to dot the chilies with half the ricotta. Evenly distribute the broccoli florets and half the jack cheese over the ricotta. Spread with ¾ cup sauce and cover with another layer of noodles. Distribute the corn and the remaining chilies, ricotta, and the cheddar evenly over the noodles. Spread ¾ cup sauce evenly over these ingredients and top with a last layer of noodles. Distribute the remaining sauce over the lasagna and sprinkle evenly with the Parmesan. Cover and bake 45 minutes. Let stand 10 minutes before serving.

Each serving provides:

384	Calories	42 g	Carbohydrate
21 g	Protein	656 mg	Sodium
15 g	Fat	49 mg	Cholesterol

Baked Macaroni and Smoked Cheese

Smoked gouda is particularly good for this dish, but smoked cheddar also yields delicious results. For good old all-British macaroni and cheese, use elbow-shaped noodles and substitute a mild cheddar for the smoked cheese.

Yield: 8 main-course servings

Lowfat milk	4	cups
Butter	3	tablespoons plus 1 teaspoon
Onion	1	medium, coarsely chopped
Flour	3	tablespoons
Dry mustard	1	tablespoon
Cayenne pepper	¼	teaspoon
Smoked cheese	½	pound, shredded
Coarse dry bread crumbs	1	cup
Parmesan cheese, finely grated	¼	cup
Dried pasta	1	pound

Recommended pasta: **elbows, penne, or other tubes**

Put several quarts of water on to boil for the pasta. Preheat oven to 375 degrees F. about 30 minutes before you are ready to bake the casserole. Warm the milk in a saucepan over very low heat. Melt 3 tablespoons of the butter over low heat in a separate heavy-bottomed saucepan or skillet. Add the onion and stir and sauté 3–4 minutes, until it begins to get limp. Add the flour and mustard and stir another minute or two, then stir in the warmed milk and cayenne. Turn the heat up to medium and cook 5–7 minutes. Add the smoked cheese and cook 3 minutes longer. The sauce will thicken slightly, but do not expect a really heavy sauce consistency. Meanwhile, cook the pasta until almost tender. You want the noodles to be still somewhat firm because they will finish cooking in the oven. Drain thoroughly. Rub a 3-quart baking dish with the remaining 1 teaspoon butter. In a large bowl, toss the pasta with the cheese sauce, then transfer to the baking dish. Combine the bread crumbs with the Parmesan and distribute this mixture evenly over the top of the casserole. Cover and bake 30 minutes, then remove cover and cook 5–10 minutes longer, until topping is crisp. Let stand at room temperature 10 minutes before serving.

Each serving provides:			
486	Calories	61 g	Carbohydrate
22 g	Protein	495 mg	Sodium
16 g	Fat	53 mg	Cholesterol

Savory Mushroom Custard with Pasta

The flavors of this casserole suggest a light cream sauce with pesto, and the texture is melt-in-your-mouth smoothness. If you have a few cups of leftover cooked noodles on hand, this is a great way to use them. When made with spinach pasta in a clear glass dish, the presentation is particularly pretty.

Yield: 8 main-course servings

Eggs	6	large
Butter	3	tablespoons
Mushrooms	1	pound, thinly sliced
Salt	¾	teaspoon
Pepper		A few grinds
Basil Pesto	3	tablespoons (see page 32)
Lowfat milk	3	cups
Dried pasta	8	ounces
Olive oil (optional)	1	tablespoon

Recommended pasta: spinach fettuccine or linguine, or 4 cups leftover cooked noodles

Preheat oven to 350 degrees F. about 30 minutes before you're ready to bake the casserole. Bring the eggs to room temperature. Unless you are using leftover noodles, cook pasta until al dente. If you are not yet ready to assemble the casserole, cool the pasta in cold water, drain, toss with a tablespoon of olive oil, and set aside. Melt the butter in a skillet. Add the mushrooms, sprinkle with ¼ teaspoon of the salt, and sauté about 8 minutes, until they have released their liquid and it has nearly evaporated. Add a little pepper and turn off the heat. Generously butter a 2-quart casserole or baking dish. In a bowl, whisk together the eggs, pesto, and the remaining ½ teaspoon salt. Warm the milk slightly in a small saucepan. Pour it into the egg mixture in a thin stream, gently whisking as you do so (milk must be only lukewarm, or it will cook the eggs). Make a layer of the noodles in the bottom of the casserole. Distribute the sautéed mushrooms over them. Evenly pour on the custard. Cover the casserole and place it in a larger baking pan that contains an inch or so of warm water. Put this arrangement into the oven and bake 45 minutes or so, until the custard is set. Let stand 10 minutes before serving.

Each serving provides:			
290	Calories	30 g	Carbohydrate
14 g	Protein	378 mg	Sodium
13 g	Fat	173 mg	Cholesterol

Couscous Casserole with Capers and Tarragon

How many years has it been since you made a casserole for guests? This recipe will open the door to a whole new realm of "meal in a dish" options. A side dish of steamed vegetables and a leafy salad is all you need to round it out. Your company will enjoy the flavors, and you will enjoy the ease of preparation and serving.

Yield: 6 main-course servings

Olive oil	4	tablespoons
Onion	1	medium, finely diced
Red bell pepper	1	medium, finely diced
Capers, drained, minced	4	teaspoons
Fresh parsley, minced	¾	cup, loosely packed
Garlic	2	medium cloves, minced
Dried tarragon	2	teaspoons
Hot water	2	cups
Dried couscous	1	cup
Lowfat milk	1	cup
Eggs	3	large
Parmesan cheese, finely grated	¾	cup

Preheat the oven to 350 degrees F. about 30 minutes before you're ready to bake the casserole. Heat 3 tablespoons of the olive oil in a 2-quart saucepan and gently sauté the onion, bell pepper, capers, parsley, garlic, and tarragon a couple of minutes. Add hot water and the couscous, bring to a boil, then cover and remove from the heat. Let stand 10 minutes. Whisk together the milk and eggs and add this and the Parmesan to the couscous mixture. Combine well. Use the remaining tablespoon of olive oil to coat a 2-quart casserole dish. Pour in the couscous mixture, cover, and bake 30 minutes.

Each serving provides:

319	Calories	29 g	Carbohydrate
14 g	Protein	336 mg	Sodium
16 g	Fat	118 mg	Cholesterol

Curried Couscous Casserole

Couscous is one of the least common pastas, but once you discover it you will begin to crave it. The texture is much different than that of other pastas, more akin to a grain. It is easy to prepare and will be complemented by many different seasonings.

Yield: 6 main-course servings

Water	2½	cups
Low-sodium vegetable broth cube	1	
Dried couscous	1	cup
Olive oil	3	tablespoons
Red bell pepper	1	medium, diced
Green onions	2	minced
Peas, fresh or frozen	1	cup
Cooked garbanzo beans	1⅓	cups
Dried tomatoes, minced	2	tablespoons
Curry powder	1	tablespoon
Salt	¼	teaspoon
Lowfat milk	¾	cup
Fresh cilantro, minced	¼	cup

Optional garnishes: lemon wedges, light sour cream, plain lowfat yogurt

Preheat oven to 350 degrees F. about 30 minutes before you are ready to bake the casserole. Heat the water and the vegetable broth cube to a boil in a 2-quart saucepan that has a tight-fitting lid. Stir in the couscous. Remove from the heat, cover, and let stand about 15 minutes. Heat 2 tablespoons of the olive oil in a small skillet over low heat. Sauté the bell pepper and green onions a minute or two. Stir in the peas, garbanzo beans, dried tomatoes, curry powder, and salt. Heat through. Stir in the milk. Mix all of this, along with the cilantro, into the cous-cous, blending well. Use the remaining tablespoon of olive oil to coat a 1½-quart casserole dish. Pour in the couscous mixture, cover, and bake 30 minutes. Serve with lemon wedges and yogurt or sour cream, if desired.

Each serving provides:			
278	Calories	42 g	Carbohydrate
11 g	Protein	151 mg	Sodium
8 g	Fat	1 mg	Cholesterol

Sauce of Mushrooms, Spinach, and Capers for Tortellini

Our friend Lori Shull created this wonderful dish. The sauce is rich, creamy, and well balanced. She usually serves it as a main course, but has also put it out with toothpicks as an appetizer.

Yield: 4 main-course servings

Neufchâtel cheese	6	ounces
Frozen chopped spinach	6	ounces
Butter	1	tablespoon
Red bell pepper	1	large, diced
Onion	1	medium, diced
Mushrooms	¼	pound, thickly sliced
Garlic	2	medium cloves, minced
Tomato	1	medium, diced
White wine	¼	cup
Parmesan cheese, finely grated	¼	cup
Capers, drained, minced	1½	tablespoons
Dried oregano	½	teaspoon
Dried basil	½	teaspoon
Fresh cheese tortellini	12	ounces

Set the Neufchâtel cheese out well ahead of time to bring it to room temperature. Thaw the spinach and drain well. Put several quarts of water on to boil for the tortellini. Melt the butter in a large skillet over low heat. Add the bell pepper, onion, mushrooms, and garlic and sauté several minutes. Add the Neufchâtel, spinach, tomato, and wine. Blend well. Mix in the

Parmesan, capers, oregano, and basil. Continue to cook until the mixture just begins to simmer, stirring constantly. Meanwhile, cook the tortellini until tender. Drain well and add to the sauce. Toss to coat and heat through. Serve in a warm bowl.

Each serving provides:

464	Calories	49 g	Carbohydrate
23 g	Protein	812 mg	Sodium
19 g	Fat	92 mg	Cholesterol

Acorn Squash Ravioli with Rosemary Walnut Sauce

This is a dish to make on a rainy Saturday afternoon. Ravioli preparation is rather time-consuming, particularly when making dough from scratch, but the results are always worth it. Make more than you need and freeze them.

Yield: 6 main-course servings

The filling

Acorn squash	1¼	pounds
Butter	2	tablespoons
Lowfat milk	1	cup
Single cream	½	cup
Freshly grated nutmeg	⅛	teaspoon
Ground cinnamon	¼	teaspoon
Salt and pepper		To taste
Honey	1	teaspoon
Basic egg noodles	1	recipe (see page 16)

The sauce

Raw walnuts, chopped	½	cup
Butter	3	tablespoons
Rosemary Pesto	2	tablespoons (see page 33)

Peel and chop the squash; you should have about 3½ cups. Place the butter and ¼ cup water in a large skillet. When the butter melts, add the squash and cook over low heat until tender, stirring occasionally, about 30 minutes. Remove from heat and mash with a potato masher. Return to the heat and stir in the milk and single cream. Cook, stirring frequently, about 20 minutes. Stir in the nutmeg, cinnamon, salt, pepper, and honey.

Prepare the pasta dough as called for in the recipe. Roll out by hand, or save time by using a pasta machine, following the manufacturer's directions. Lay out strips of pasta about 2 inches wide and 10 inches long, in pairs. On one of each pair of noodles place about a teaspoon of the squash filling every 1½ inches, going the length of the pasta. Put a few drops of water on your finger and draw a square around each mound of filling to moisten the dough. Cover the entire strip with another noodle and press the dough down firmly with your fingers to seal around each mound, pushing out any air as you do this. Slice through the dough to create individual ravioli. Continue this process until all the filling and dough are used up. As you complete them, wrap the ravioli in a lightly floured tea towel until ready to cook, so they do not dry out. Meanwhile, heat several quarts of water to a rapid boil and add a tablespoon of oil. Cook the ravioli 5–8 minutes, until tender.

While they are cooking, gently toast the chopped walnuts (see page 20). Melt the butter in a small pan and add the Rosemary Pesto; heat through. Serve the ravioli on warm plates drizzled with the sauce. Sprinkle with the walnuts.

Each serving provides:

482	Calories	49 g	Carbohydrate
13 g	Protein	364 mg	Sodium
27 g	Fat	142 mg	Cholesterol

Spinach Nutmeg Ravioli
with Tomato and Brandy Cream

This is really a shortcut ravioli recipe because the noodle is the commercially prepared fresh round wonton wrapper. You can also make this dish with fresh homemade pasta, if you have an abundance of time.

Yield: 6 main-course servings

The sauce

Tomato sauce	1	16-ounce can
Single cream	1	cup
Freshly grated nutmeg	⅛	teaspoon
Brandy	¼	cup

The filling

Frozen chopped spinach	10	ounces
Butter	3	tablespoons
Onion	1	small, finely diced
Garlic	2	medium cloves, minced
Freshly grated nutmeg	⅛	teaspoon
Lowfat milk	¼	cup
Part-skim ricotta cheese	8	ounces
Fresh round wonton wrappers	12	ounces

Ahead of time, thaw the spinach and drain well. Combine the tomato sauce, single cream, and ⅛ teaspoon nutmeg in a skillet. Bring to a simmer and cook about 10 minutes, stirring often. Add the brandy and heat through, then set aside.

To make the filling, melt the butter in a skillet and sauté the onion, garlic, and ⅛ teaspoon nutmeg 2–3 minutes. Stir in the spinach and milk. Add the ricotta, mixing well. Turn off the heat.

To assemble the ravioli, place a wonton wrapper on a floured work surface. Place a scant teaspoonful of the spinach mixture on one side. Dip your finger in water and draw a line around the outer edge of the noodle. Fold over and seal tightly, pressing out any trapped air as you go. Wrap the filled ravioli in a lightly floured tea towel so they do not dry out. Continue this process until you have filled all the wrappers. Bring several quarts of water to a boil and cook the ravioli until tender. Briefly reheat the sauce while they are cooking. Serve the ravioli on heated plates with the sauce drizzled over the top.

	Each serving provides:		
379	Calories	43 g	Carbohydrate
15 g	Protein	635 mg	Sodium
14 g	Fat	42 mg	Cholesterol

Oregano Pesto Manicotti

Oregano pesto has a flavor all its own. It is worth making for this dish, but you can substitute basil pesto if you have some on hand. The presentation is festive and the flavors a delight.

Yield: 6 main-course servings

The sauce

Olive oil	2	tablespoons
Garlic	2	medium cloves, minced
Onion	1	medium, diced
Stewed tomatoes	1	28-ounce can
Fresh oregano leaves	2	tablespoons
Lemon	2	slices
Bay leaves	3	
Port	2	tablespoons

The filling

Firm-style tofu	6	ounces
Part-skim ricotta cheese	1	cup
Light sour cream	¾	cup
Egg	1	large, beaten
Oregano Pesto	1	cup (see page 36)
Part-skim mozzarella cheese, shredded	1	cup
Parmesan cheese, finely grated	½	cup
Olive oil	1	tablespoon
Dried manicotti noodles	8	ounces

Preheat the oven to 350 degrees F. about 30 minutes before you are ready to bake the manicotti. Heat 2 tablespoons olive oil in a large pan and sauté the garlic and onion several minutes. Add the tomatoes, oregano, lemon slices, and bay leaves. Cook over medium-high heat about 30 minutes, stirring occasionally. Reduce the heat and add the port. Cook about 15 minutes longer, until the sauce is rather thick. Turn off the heat and set aside.

Meanwhile, cook the manicotti noodles in a very large pot of water until almost al dente. They need lots of room to swim around while cooking, so prepare in two batches if necessary. The noodles must be undercooked in order to stuff them. They will finish cooking in the oven. Drain and rinse the noodles and lay them on a tea towel to dry. Slice the tofu and blot with a tea towel to remove surface moisture. Mash in a large bowl with a potato masher or fork. Add the ricotta, sour cream, egg, and pesto. Combine well. Add the mozzarella and Parmesan and stir to incorporate. Stuff each noodle with the cheese mixture; a baby spoon works well for this. Rub a 9 × 13-inch baking dish with 1 tablespoon olive oil. Arrange the stuffed manicotti in the pan in a single layer. Spoon the tomato sauce over them along their center and bake, covered, 35 minutes.

Each serving provides:			
676	Calories	47 g	Carbohydrate
30 g	Protein	486 mg	Sodium
42 g	Fat	72 mg	Cholesterol

Tofu Pesto Rollups

In this dish the noodles are rolled up jelly-roll fashion, which makes a very nice presentation with the multicolored fillings and the curly edges of the noodles. If you are short of time, you can substitute a store-bought marinara sauce for the Tomato Sauce with Fresh Oregano. For this dish, avoid whole wheat lasagna varieties as they break apart too easily. Be sure to gauge the amount of filling in each rollup carefully, so you will have enough for 12 noodles (you may wish to cook a few extra noodles, in case some break).

Yield: 6 main-course servings

Firm-style tofu	6	ounces
Part-skim ricotta cheese	1	cup
Light sour cream	½	cup
Basil Pesto	½	cup (see page 32)
Garlic	3	medium cloves, minced
Olive oil	1	tablespoon
Tomato Sauce with Fresh Oregano	1½	cups (see page 176)
Parmesan cheese, finely grated	½	cup
Dried semolina lasagna noodles	8	ounces

Preheat the oven to 350 degrees F. Bring a large pan of water to a boil for the noodles, as they need plenty of room to swim around in while cooking. Cook the noodles until almost tender. They will finish cooking as they bake. Remove very gently from the water, rinse under cold water, drain well, and place on a tea towel to dry. (You want to remove as much of the water as possible.) Slice the tofu and blot with a tea towel to remove surface water. Mash it in a mixing bowl with a fork or potato masher.

Add the ricotta, sour cream, pesto, and garlic and combine thoroughly. Spread about a ¼-inch layer of the mixture along the entire length and width of each noodle and roll up. Rub a 9 × 13-inch baking dish with the olive oil. Place the rollups in the dish seam side down. Top them with the sauce and Parmesan. Bake uncovered for 25 minutes and serve immediately.

Each serving provides:			
471	Calories	44 g	Carbohydrate
24 g	Protein	590 mg	Sodium
24 g	Fat	24 mg	Cholesterol

Pesto Ricotta Shells with Herbed Tomato Sauce

These jumbo shells look so charming when they are served, and they taste wonderful!

Yield: 6 main-course servings

The sauce

Fresh pear tomatoes	1½	pounds
Olive oil	1	tablespoon
Onion	1	small, minced
Garlic	2	medium cloves, minced
Lemon	1	slice
Fresh oregano leaves	1	tablespoon
Fresh chives, minced	1	tablespoon
White wine	½	cup

The filling

Egg	1	large
Part-skim ricotta cheese	1	cup
Basil Pesto	1	cup (see page 32)
Parmesan cheese, finely grated	½	cup
Dried jumbo pasta shells	8	ounces

Preheat the oven to 350 degrees F. about 30 minutes before you are ready to bake the shells. Blanch, peel, and seed the tomatoes (see page 20) and chop coarsely. Heat the olive oil in a large pan and sauté the onion and garlic a minute or two. Add the tomatoes and lemon. Simmer over low heat 15 minutes, then crush the tomatoes with a wooden spoon and stir in the herbs and wine. Continue to cook until reduced to a thick sauce consistency.

Bring several quarts of water to a boil. Add a little olive oil and cook the shells until almost tender, stirring frequently so they do not stick to the bottom of the pan or each other. They will finish cooking in the oven. Lift them into a colander and rinse with cold water. Drain well. Beat the egg and whisk in the ricotta and pesto. Stir in the Parmesan. Spoon half the tomato sauce into a 9 × 13-inch baking dish. Fill each shell with some of the ricotta mixture and place in the baking dish. Spoon remaining sauce over them, bake uncovered 20 minutes, and serve immediately.

	Each serving provides:		
531	Calories	46 g	Carbohydrate
23 g	Protein	458 mg	Sodium
29 g	Fat	64 mg	Cholesterol

Shells Filled with
Dried Tomatoes and Pesto

This dish is wonderful for a summer party. The shells are served at room temperature so the oven does not heat up the kitchen. Or serve them during the winter holiday season as an appetizer. The red and green colors fit in perfectly with that time of year.

Yield: 8 main-course servings

Neufchâtel cheese	16	ounces
Olive oil	1	tablespoon
Firm-style tofu	4	ounces
Part-skim ricotta cheese	1	cup
Garlic	4	medium cloves, minced
Basil Pesto	¾	cup (see page 32)
Dried tomatoes, minced	½	cup
Salt and pepper		To taste
Pine nuts	½	cup
Fresh parsley (for garnish)		Many sprigs
Dried jumbo pasta shells	32–36	

Well ahead of time, set the Neufchâtel cheese out to bring it to room temperature. Bring several quarts of water with a little oil in it to a boil and cook the shells until al dente, stirring frequently so they do not stick to the bottom of the pan or to each other. Drain well. Refill the pan with cold water and add the olive oil, then stir in the cooked pasta to cool. The olive oil will prevent the shells from sticking together. When cool, drain again and gently shake to remove all the water. Set shells aside to dry on a tea towel.

The Best 125 Meatless Pasta Dishes

Meanwhile, slice the tofu and blot the slices with a tea towel to remove surface water. Mash it in a bowl with a potato masher or fork. Mix in the Neufchâtel cheese, ricotta, garlic, pesto, and dried tomatoes until creamy in texture. Season with salt and pepper. Toast the pine nuts (see page 20). To stuff the shells, hold open in the palm of your hand and spoon in the filling. Arrange the filled shells on a serving platter. Top each one with a couple of pine nuts and a parsley sprig. Refrigerate several hours. Bring to room temperature before serving.

Each serving provides:

591	Calories	50 g	Carbohydrate
25 g	Protein	408 mg	Sodium
35 g	Fat	58 mg	Cholesterol

Spinach Lasagna with Port

This lasagna is fairly traditional in flavor and composition, except for the subtle accent of the port. Prepare this dish when you are feeding a crowd, as everything can be done ahead. Add garlic bread and a big green salad and you are ready to feast. Lasagna also freezes well, so one pan of this could be put away for a future meal.

Yield: 16 main-dish servings

The sauce

Olive oil	3	tablespoons
Onions	2	medium, coarsely chopped
Celery, diced	1	cup
Garlic	3	medium cloves, minced
Chopped black olives	1	4½-ounce can
Lemon	2	slices
Crushed tomatoes	2	28-ounce cans
Dried oregano	1	tablespoon
Dried basil	1	tablespoon
Bay leaves	4	
Salt	¼	teaspoon
Pepper	⅛	teaspoon
Port	¾	cup

The filling

Fresh spinach	2	bunches (about 1½ pounds)
Firm-style tofu	6	ounces
Part-skim ricotta cheese	2½	cups
Light sour cream	1	cup
Eggs	3	large, beaten

Fresh parsley, minced	1	cup
Dried oregano	1	tablespoon
Dried basil	1	tablespoon
Salt and pepper		to taste
Part-skim mozzarella cheese, shredded	3½	cups
Parmesan cheese, finely grated	1	cup
Dried lasagna noodles	1	pound
Olive oil	2	tablespoons

Preheat the oven to 350 degrees F. about 30 minutes before you are ready to bake the lasagna. Heat the olive oil in a large pan and sauté the onion, celery, and garlic a few minutes. Add the olives, lemon slices, and tomatoes, then stir in the oregano, basil, bay leaves, salt, and pepper. Simmer over low heat 30–40 minutes, stirring occasionally. Add the port during the last 15 minutes of cooking.

While the sauce is cooking you can prepare the filling. Carefully wash the spinach, remove the stems, and place the leaves in a steamer rack over a couple of inches of boiling water in a lidded pot. Steam until it wilts. Place the cooked spinach in a colander to cool. Squeeze to remove as much water as possible; set aside. Slice the tofu and blot with a tea towel to remove surface water. Mash the tofu in a mixing bowl with a fork or potato masher. Stir in the ricotta, sour cream, eggs, parsley, oregano, basil, salt, and pepper and combine well. Bring a huge quantity of water to a boil in a very large pot and cook the noodles until almost al dente. (Lasagna noodles need lots of room to swim around freely as they cook, so if you don't have a huge pot, cook them in batches.) The noodles will finish cooking in the oven. Cool them in a bowl of cold water, drain, and place on a tea towel until you need them. Oil two 9 × 13-inch glass baking dishes with 1 tablespoon olive oil each. Layer the

Baked and Stuffed Pasta   289

ingredients as follows: sauce, noodles, spinach, ricotta mixture, noodles, mozzarella, sauce, Parmesan. Cover with foil and bake 45 minutes. Remove the foil and bake 5 minutes longer. The sauce should be bubbling hot and the top slightly brown. Let stand about 10 minutes before cutting.

Each serving provides:

358	Calories	34 g	Carbohydrate
22 g	Protein	591 mg	Sodium
15 g	Fat	71 mg	Cholesterol

Porcini, Mustard, and Ricotta Ravioli with Lemon Oregano Cream

*Making ravioli from scratch is a labor of love and dinner guests are
sure to be impressed by your devotion. If you aren't interested in
practicing this art, you can use fresh wonton wrappers from the
supermarket. Homemade is preferable, but either way the flavors of
the filling and the sauce make for a very special meal.*

Yield: 6 main-course servings

The filling

Dried porcini mushrooms	1	ounce
Mustard greens	1	bunch (about ¾ pound)
Butter	2	tablespoons
Garlic	3	medium cloves, minced
Fresh oregano leaves	1	tablespoon
Part-skim ricotta cheese	1	cup
Salt	½	teaspoon
Pepper		Several grinds
Basic egg noodles	1	recipe (see page 16)
Olive oil	1	tablespoon

The sauce

Sesame seeds	1	tablespoon
Butter	2	tablespoons
Salt	¼	teaspoon
Lemon juice	2	tablespoons
Single cream	½	cup
Flour	1	tablespoon
Fresh oregano leaves	1	tablespoon

Soak the porcini in 2 cups hot water for 30 minutes or so. Lift out the mushrooms. Strain the soaking liquid through a paper coffee filter to remove any grit and set aside. Coarsely chop the mushrooms. Wash and dry the mustard greens, chop coarsely, and set aside. In a high-walled skillet, melt the butter over low heat. Add the garlic and 1 tablespoon fresh oregano. Stir and sauté a minute or two, then add the chopped mushrooms. Stir and sauté 3–4 minutes longer, then add the mustard greens all at once, along with 2 tablespoons of mushroom soaking liquid. Put a tight lid on the pot and cook over low heat 7–8 minutes, until greens are wilted and tender. Spoon this mixture into a food processor and pulse to chop finely, or mince by hand. In a bowl, stir this mixture into the ricotta. Add the salt and pepper, and stir again to distribute everything evenly.

Prepare the dough as called for in the recipe. Roll out by hand, or save time by using a pasta machine, following the manufacturer's directions. Lay out strips of pasta about 2 inches wide and 10 inches long, in pairs. On one of each pair of noodles, place about a teaspoon of the filling every 1½ inches, going the length of the pasta. Put a few drops of water on your finger and draw a square around each mound of filling to moisten the dough. Cover the entire strip with another noodle and press the dough down firmly with your fingers to seal around each mound, pushing out any air as you do this. Slice through the dough to create individual ravioli. Continue this process until all the filling and dough are used up. As you complete them, wrap the ravioli in a lightly floured tea towel until ready to cook, so they do not dry out. Meanwhile, bring several quarts of water to a rapid boil and add a tablespoon of oil. Cook the ravioli 6–8 minutes, until tender.

While they are cooking, toast the sesame seeds (see page 20) and set aside. Heat 1 cup of the mushroom soaking liquid with the butter and salt in a small saucepan over low heat. When simmering, whisk in the lemon juice, then the single cream. Vigorously shake the flour with 3 tablespoons water in a small lidded jar. When the sauce is again simmering, whisk in the flour and water mixture. Simmer and whisk over medium heat about 5 minutes, until sauce thickens a little. Turn off the heat and stir in the oregano. Serve the ravioli very hot with a bit of the sauce drizzled over them. Sprinkle with toasted sesame seeds to provide a nice light crunch.

Each serving provides:

413	Calories	46 g	Carbohydrate
16 g	Protein	641 mg	Sodium
19 g	Fat	147 mg	Cholesterol

Garden Basket Lasagna

This lasagna is just like Mom used to make, but without the meat! The flavors are pure and simple and the texture rich and cheesy. To keep the sodium level of this dish reasonable, be sure to use a salt-free variety of canned tomatoes.

Yield: 8 main-course servings

The sauce

Olive oil	3	tablespoons
Onions	3	medium, coarsely chopped
Garlic	3	medium cloves, minced
Tomato paste	2	6-ounce cans
Low-sodium whole tomatoes	2	28-ounce cans
Fresh parsley, minced	1	cup
Dried oregano	2	teaspoons
Dried basil	2	teaspoons
Bay leaves	3	
Lemon	2	slices
Salt	¼	teaspoon
Pepper		A few grinds

The filling

Caraway seeds	1	tablespoon
Part-skim ricotta cheese	15	ounces
Light sour cream	1	cup
Olive oil	1	tablespoon
Zucchini	2	medium, thinly sliced
Yellow squash	2	medium, thinly sliced
Green bell pepper	2	medium, thinly sliced

Part-skim mozzarella cheese	8	ounces, shredded
Parmesan cheese, finely grated	½	cup
Dried lasagna noodles	8	ounces
Olive oil	1	tablespoon

About 30 minutes before baking, preheat the oven to 350 degrees F. Heat the olive oil in a large skillet and sauté the onions and garlic several minutes. Add the tomato paste and chopped canned tomatoes, discarding the juice drained from one of the cans, but including the juice from the other. Bring to a simmer and add the parsley, oregano, basil, bay leaves, lemon slices, salt, and pepper. Simmer uncovered over low heat about 1 hour, stirring occasionally, until the sauce is considerably reduced. Meanwhile, bring several quarts of water to a boil and cook the pasta until almost al dente. It will finish cooking in the oven. Cool the noodles in a bowl of cold water, drain, and place on a tea towel to dry until you need them.

Toast the caraway seeds (see page 20) and mix them with the ricotta and sour cream. Rub a 9 × 13-inch baking dish with 1 tablespoon olive oil. Put ¼ of the tomato sauce on the bottom, then add a layer of sliced vegetables, then a layer of noodles. Dot with some of the ricotta mixture and sprinkle on some mozzarella. Repeat the layers 2 or 3 times. Top with the Parmesan. Cover with foil and bake 45 minutes. Uncover and bake 10 minutes longer. Let stand at room temperature 10 minutes before serving.

Each serving provides:

443	Calories	50 g	Carbohydrate
24 g	Protein	750 mg	Sodium
18 g	Fat	38 mg	Cholesterol

Cooking Up a
Healthier Planet

Perhaps you feel you've heard enough about saving the planet.
You may have read all the books and magazines, seen all the
programs on television. Perhaps you think you know it all.

But just knowing isn't enough. Are you feeling it yet—out-
rage at the abuses, grief at the losses, righteous determination
to help preserve what's left of the diversity and integrity of our
ecosystem?

Many of us have chosen to avoid the issues—closed our
minds and hearts to the barrage of data. Too much bad news,

too many overwhelming challenges, too painful! What, after all, can we do about it?

Well, here comes the good news. Massive healing is made of minuscule changes. Every decision we make as consumers, every discussion we have with friends, all of our smallest and most mundane habits make a difference. Like cells in this huge living organism called Earth, every word or act—every choice—is either diseased or healthy, part of the problem or part of the solution.

So cooks, take heart and take responsibility. Let's make our choices—at the market, in the kitchen, in the garden— healthy ones. Here are just a few ways we as cooks can help save the world:

- Buy organic. The statistics on pesticide-related pollution of our air, water, and food are horrifying. We don't yet know the cumulative effect of a lifetime of eating chemical-laden foods—those of us now living are guinea pigs—but the preliminary signs are not encouraging. There is no question that pesticides are unhealthy for our bodies and for the planet. Demonstrate your concern and commitment by paying a little extra for organic produce. Request that your grocer carry organic foods. It is only through widespread consumer demand that we will see healthier farming practices and lower organic food prices. Better yet, have fun growing your own organic food, or buy from local organic farmers.

- Eat low on the food chain. There are health risks associated with meat eating beyond the much-publicized heart disease connection. Quite a large percentage of all the antibiotics produced in the United Kingdom annually is fed to livestock, and residues remain in the meat you see in the supermarket case. In addition, salmonella contamination is found in 50–80 percent of all broilers and is also known to be present in some eggs in the United Kingdom.

From an environmental perspective, consider that it takes between 22 and 44 times less fossil fuel to produce beans and grains than to produce meat. In addition, an estimated 85 percent of our topsoil erosion is associated with raising livestock.

If you have humanitarian leanings, you will be impressed by statistics suggesting that vastly more people can be fed from an acre of land devoted to grain cultivation rather than livestock grazing. There are other ethical concerns to consider—for instance, many people consciously demonstrate their respect for all life by declining to eat animals.

Whatever your stand on these challenging issues, it makes sense for your health and the planet's health to switch to a grain- and vegetable-based diet—including lots of meatless pasta!

- Minimize or eliminate packaging: pre-cycle. The first simple step is to purchase a basket or cloth bag for carrying groceries home. Plastic bags won't decompose in the landfill, and the ink used to print on them emits dangerous toxins when burned. Paper bags are biodegradable, but not a truly responsible option because they're made from trees. Choosing paper over plastic packaging is good, but buying food in bulk and taking it home in your own containers (like reused glass jars) is much better.

- Buy unbleached paper products—and minimize their use. White paper used to make coffee filters, paper towels, toilet paper, and the like is bleached, and the bleaching process creates dioxin, a deadly toxin now polluting our water. Rethink your consumption of plastic wraps. They are laden with potentially harmful chemicals that may leach into food, and they linger a long time in the landfill. Store food in the refrigerator in reusable containers. Clean up with rags instead of paper towels. Use wax paper, which is biodegradable, instead of plastic or foil when disposable wraps are unavoidable.

- Conserve energy in the kitchen. Check the temperature of your refrigerator and freezer—just a few degrees colder than necessary can substantially increase your energy consumption. Refrigerator temperature should be between 38 and 42 degrees Fahrenheit, the freezer between 0 and 5 degrees Fahrenheit. When you shop for a gas cooker, remember that an electronic ignition system will use about 40 percent less gas than a pilot light. Use a pipe cleaner to keep gas ports unclogged on your burners. For reheating items or baking small quantities, use a top oven rather than your larger oven. Better yet, invest in a solar box cooker. They're simple to build from inexpensive materials and they cook food absolutely free of charge. The environment also pays no price when we let the sun do the cooking. For information about how to build your own solar box cooker, contact Solar Box Cookers International, 1724 11th St., Sacramento, CA 95814.

- Don't waste water. The story of water use and abuse, and their effects on our ecosystem is complex. Here, suffice it to say that when we waste water in our homes we contribute to chemical pollution and to the need for dams, which have a very serious impact on the health of our rivers and land. Kitchens are, by nature, water intensive. We need to wash most foods, we cook many foods in water, and we use great quantities of the stuff in cleaning up after meals. This doesn't include the water we simply drink—perhaps the most justifiable of all our water uses. If you grow some of your own food, your garden is another heavy water consumer.

  There are many simple steps you can take to reduce your garden and kitchen water consumption. First and foremost, don't turn on the tap and simply let water flow down the drain. Fill a bowl or bucket with water and use it to wash vegetables, rather than running the tap. This "gray water" can be used again, with the addition of soap, for washing dishes or wiping down counters and floors. Collect all water you use in the kitchen that has not been salted or harshly soaped and water plants with it. (Pasta cooking water can be recycled this way only if you choose not to salt the pot.) When cleaning up, wash and rinse in basins instead of letting the water flow. Another great water saver is to cool foods by placing them in a bowl of cold, even iced, water rather than letting cold tap water run over them. This is an excellent method for stopping the cooking of pasta, vegetables, and the like, if you do not want to keep them warm after cooking. Then you can reuse the water in the garden or for some other purpose.

- Minimize garbage production. We Americans are a wasteful lot, encouraged by the throwaway ethic of a consumer society. In many parts of the country, however, the seriousness of garbage proliferation is painfully apparent. Landfills are loaded and there simply isn't any place for the garbage to go. Fortunately, we can have a great deal of impact on this situation. Recycling has caught on nationwide as a method for reducing solid waste, while at the same time saving on the cost of producing new packaging materials. If the sanitation department of your city or town doesn't yet offer curbside recycling, bring pressure to bear on the policymakers so it will be instituted. Meanwhile, do some research to discover whether there are companies nearby that buy recycled materials and get together with your neighbors to collect them. It is possible you could earn a little money by gathering recyclables and transporting them to the collection site. Newspapers and other paper products, aluminum and tin cans, glass of all types, waxed milk cartons, and many types of plastic—even Styrofoam—can be recycled in many areas.

Kitchen food scraps constitute a good proportion of the solid wastes at our landfills. If you grow a garden and don't collect food scraps for composting, you are throwing away great organic soil enrichers. Check your library for books that describe the very simple process of composting garbage to create rich humus for your plants. You will experience the great satisfaction of applying potential garbage to useful purposes, and you will save money on commercial fertilizer preparations. The joy of compost is just one more reason to grow a garden!

Recommended

Bonar, Anne. *Vegetables: A complete guide to the cultivation, uses and nutritional value of common and exotic vegetables*. Twickenham: Hamlyn, 1986.

British Heart Foundation. *Diet and Your Heart*. London: British Heart Foundation, 1980.

Brown, Sarah. *Healthy Living Cookbook*. London: Dorling Kindersley, 1991.

Dyson, Katie (ed.). *Cooking for Your Heart's Content: The official British Heart Foundation cookbook*. London: Hutchinson, 1976.

Elliot, Rose. *Health and Happiness Through the Food You Eat*. Liss: White Eagle, 1982.

Garber, Sonja. *A Taste of Health*. London: Robert Hale, 1981.

Goldbeck, Nicki. *Cooking What Comes Naturally*. Wellingborough: Thorsons in cooperation with the Vegetarian Society of Great Britain, 1985.

Haas, Robert. *Eat to Win*. Harmondsworth: Penguin Books, 1986.

Hallinan, Beth. *Wholehearted Cooking*. London: Arrow Books, 1991.

Hunt, Janet. *The Green Cook's Encyclopedia*. London: Green Print, 1991.

Lindsay, Anne. *The Lighthearted Cookbook*. London: Grub Street in association with the British Heart Foundation, 1991.

Oddy, Derek J. and Miller, Derek S. (eds.). *Diet and Health in Modern Britain*. London: Croom Helm, 1985.

Spencer, Colin. *The New Vegetarian*. London: Gaia Books, 1992.

Whittet, Annabel (ed.). *The Vegetarian Good Food Guide*. London: The Consumers' Association/Hodder & Stoughton, 1990.

Index

sauce, sweet and sour, 146
spicy, salad with calamata
olives, 102
spinach and, with dried
tomatoes and feta, 156
spinach, lasagna, 260
in tempeh and veggies with
miso tahini sauce, 162
Avocado(s)
in pasta salad Mexicana, 118
in Mexican pasta, 204
pasta with cilantro pesto
and, 135
salsa, spicy zucchini noodle
soup with, 62
tomato Madeira sauce with,
200

B

Baked and stuffed pasta. *See*
Contents for list of
recipe titles
recipes, 259–295
tips on, 257–258
Balsamic vinegar
about, 88
in cold vermicelli with
roasted tomatoes, fresh
basil, and eggs, 114
in creamy pasta with
artichokes and dried
tomatoes, 224
in grilled vegetables in
dried-tomato marinade,
152
in pasta salad Mexicana, 118
in spicy aubergine pasta
salad with calamata
olives, 102
Basil, fresh. *See also* Basil pesto

angel hair with tomatoes
and, 180
in creamy aubergine and
Gorgonzola sauce, 250
and eggs, cold vermicelli
with roasted tomatoes,
and, 114
in pasta carbonara senza
carne, 218
in pasta primavera, 192
in savory ricotta sauce, 236
in spinach aubergine
lasagna, 260
summer squash with, and
Madeira, 154
Basil pesto, 32
light tomato cream with, 184
pasta al, frittata, 263
in pasta with, potatoes, and
green beans, 142
and pasta, salad of olives,
artichokes, and, 106
pasta salad with, and peas, 94
ricotta shells with herbed
tomato sauce, 284
in savory mushroom custard
with pasta, 268
shells filled with dried
tomatoes and, 286
in summer-fresh pasta salad,
90
in tofu pesto rollups, 282
tomato pesto pasta, 177
tortellini soup with, 65
in two-bean zuppa, 82
Beans. *See also* Adzuki beans,
Cannellini beans,
Garbanzo beans, Green
beans, Kidney beans,
Lima beans

Mustard seeds
  in couscous salad with
      dried-tomato vinai-
      grette, 122
  pasta salad with broccoli
      and, 92

N

Neufchâtel cheese
  in sauce of mushrooms,
      spinach, and capers for
      tortellini, 274
  in shells filled with dried
      tomatoes and pesto, 286
Nutrition alert, 22–25
Nut(s). *See also* Almonds,
      Cashews, Peanuts,
      Pecans, Pine nuts,
      Walnuts
  about, 8–9
  toasting, 20
Nutmeg
  cream, leeks, carrots and
      pecans in, 216
  ricotta with, and peas, 234

O

Oil(s)
  calories in, 23
  canola, about, 2
  olive, about, 2
  roasted sesame, about, 2
Olive(s)
  artichokes, pesto, and pasta,
      salad of, 106
  calamata, spicy aubergine
      salad with, 102
  calamata, spicy tomato sauce
      with arugula and, 194
  in dried-tomato carbonara,
      132

in Greek-style pasta salad
    with tarragon, 110
lentil, feta and pasta salad,
    108
in pasta oliveto, 182
in pasta salad Mexicana, 118
and pimiento pesto, 38
in pizza pasta, 138
in spinach lasagna with port,
    288
in Tex-Mex tofu and noodles,
    198
in tomato and lentil sauce
    with feta, 208
in tomato Madeira sauce
    with avocado, 198
and tomato pesto, 40
Onion(s)
  in garden basket lasagna, 294
  in pasta carbonara senza
      carne, 218
  soup with pasta, French, 68
  tomatoes with sweet
      rosemary, 188
Oregano, fresh
  lemon cream, porcini,
      mustard, and ricotta
      ravioli with, 291
  in sauce of feta, fresh herbs,
      and cashews, 248
  tomato sauce with, 176
Oregano pesto, 36
  manicotti, 280
Oyster mushrooms, with
      cilantro and cream, 220

P

Parsley
  about, 5
  in cilantro pesto, 34

Shiitake mushrooms
  about, 8
  fresh, angel hair with
      tomatoes and, 190
  spicy brussels sprouts
      with baby corn and,
      158
  spicy greens with adzuki
      beans and, 168
  and spinach pesto with
      ginger, 44
Smoked cheese, baked
      macaroni and, 266
Soba
  in broth with fried vegeta-
      bles and *age*, 66
  salad with carrots,
      mangetout peas, and
      sesame mayo, 116
  sesame, with burdock root
      and carrot, 166
Sodium, about, 24–25
Soups with pasta. *See* Contents
      for list of recipe titles
  recipes, 50–85
  tips on, 47–49
Spinach
  and aubergine with dried
      tomato and feta, 156
  and cheese pesto with
      pimiento, 42
  and shiitake pesto with
      ginger, 44
  aubergine lasagna, 260
  lasagna with port, 288
  lima bean, and pasta soup, 78
  nutmeg ravioli in tomato and
      brandy cream, 278
  sauce of mushrooms, and
      capers for tortellini, 274
  soup with stars, cream of, 54

Sunflower seeds
  in green chili sauce with sour
      cream, 242
  in pasta salad Mexicana, 118
  in spicy brussels sprouts
      with baby corn and
      shiitake, 158
  toasting, 20

T
Tahini
  about, 9
  in hot baba ghanoush with
      pasta, 160
  sauce, tempeh and veggies
      with miso, 162
Tarragon
  citrus dressing, mushrooms,
      Jarlsburg and pasta
      with, 96
  couscous casserole with
      capers and, 270
  cream, asparagus and
      mushrooms in, 222
  creamy red bell pepper
      sauce with, 238
  Greek-style pasta salad with,
      112
  tomato sauce with, and
      capers, 186
Tempeh
  about, 10
  curried tomato sauce with
      peanuts and, 206
  and veggies with miso tahini
      sauce, 162
Toasting seeds and nuts, 20
Tofu
  about, 10
  in oregano pesto manicotti,
      280